Educational Research and Innovation

Back to the Future of Education

FOUR OECD SCENARIOS FOR SCHOOLING

OECD

BETTER POLICIES FOR BETTER LIVES

This work is published under the responsibility of the Secretary-General of the OECD. The opinions expressed and arguments employed herein do not necessarily reflect the official views of OECD member countries.

This document, as well as any data and map included herein, are without prejudice to the status of or sovereignty over any territory, to the delimitation of international frontiers and boundaries and to the name of any territory, city or area.

Please cite this publication as:
OECD (2020), *Back to the Future of Education: Four OECD Scenarios for Schooling*, Educational Research and Innovation, OECD Publishing, Paris, *https://doi.org/10.1787/178ef527-en*.

ISBN 978-92-64-95813-5 (print)
ISBN 978-92-64-96753-3 (pdf)
ISBN 978-92-64-44396-9 (HTML)
ISBN 978-92-64-36932-0 (epub)

Educational Research and Innovation
ISSN 2076-9660 (print)
ISSN 2076-9679 (online)

Foreword

2020, this evocative year of hindsight and foresight, has humbled us with a global shock: the COVID-19 pandemic. We have been reminded that, despite the best laid plans, the truth is that the future likes to surprise us. To prepare our education systems for what may come, we have to consider not only the changes that appear most probable, but also the ones that we are not expecting.

There are always multiple versions of the future – some are assumptions, others hopes and fears, or even signals that something is already changing. *Back to the future of education: Four OECD Scenarios for Schooling* provides a set of scenarios on the future of schooling to support long-term strategic thinking in education. These scenarios, which build on the 2001 edition, show us that there is not a single path into the future, but many.

This volume is a companion volume to the *Trends Shaping Education* series, a triannual publication that highlights key global megatrends and their potential impact on education. While megatrends focus on patterns from the past to inspire thinking about the future, scenarios allow us to consider newly emerging patterns and possibilities.

A key question for thinking about the future of education is: To what extent are our current structures helping or hindering our vision? Put another way, if today we were to meet with a Martian, freshly arrived on planet earth and looking for tips on designing their own education system, what would we suggest?

Would we suggest starting with schools and schooling as we know them now and advise modernising and fine-tuning the system, the conceptual equivalent of reconfiguring windows and doors of a house? Or would we rather recommend an entirely different way to use the people, spaces, time and technology? Who would be involved in these processes of transformation, and how much of the lifespan would it encompass (infancy? early childhood? adulthood, aligned to labour market? Or lifelong, including learning for our eldest seniors at 80 and 90+ years, a growing cohort as our populations age?)?

The path forward is likely a combination of these two approaches. Revisioning and transforming education is a powerful tool, pushing us to think outside of the box and to go beyond our current limitations. So too is building on what we have, modernising the trusted institutions that play such an important role in the social fabric of our communities and societies.

By using schools and schooling as a starting point, this volume and the four scenarios within it open the door to both approaches. They can be used to inspire, to dream, to transform. They can be used to future-proof systems and stress-test against unexpected shocks. Above all, they push us to move beyond complacency and easy solutions, presenting us with the tensions and paradoxes inherent in all our systems and which we must address. We hope you enjoy the journey. Use them in good health.

Andreas Schleicher

Andreas Schleicher
Director for Education and Skills
Special Advisor on Education Policy to the Secretary-General

Acknowledgements

This book stems from and was inspired by past Centre for Educational Research and Innovation (CERI) work, from the original *Schooling for Tomorrow* scenarios, first published in 2001, to over a decade of work on *Trends Shaping Education* thereafter. We are indebted to David Istance, for many years a pillar of CERI and the leader of the transformative *Schooling for Tomorrow* and *Innovative Learning Environments* projects, as well as the author, along with Henno Theisens, of *Trends Shaping Education 2008*, the first edition in that highly successful series.

In addition, the authors would like to thank Petra Packalen (Finnish National Agency for Education, and a contributor to Trends Shaping Education 2008) and Liana Tang (Centre for Strategic Futures, Prime Minister's Office, Singapore) for generously providing examples of how future thinking works in the practice of national education policy. We would also like to thank our colleagues Duncan Cass-Beggs and Joshua Polchar of the OECD Foresight Unit, for sharing their futures thinking expertise and working with us during the writing of this report. We also want to acknowledge Guim Tió's generous help with the book cover. Thank you.

The ideas compiled in this book benefited from many other projects within CERI and the wider OECD Directorate for Education and Skills. We would like to thank all of our bright colleagues, whose rigorous work made this analysis possible.

In addition, the authors would like to thank present and past colleagues who provided expert ideas and suggestions for improvement, to this volume as well as the overall process of developing these scenarios and our capacity to think more systematically about the future. From brainstorming analytical approaches to actively stress-testing versions of scenarios, we thank Liam Bekirsky, Mollie Dollinger, Manuela Fitzpatrick, Francesca Gottschalk, Marissa Miller, Joshua Polchar, Nóra Révai, Dhiman Talapatra, Hannah Ulferts and Ziyin Xiong as well as the numerous internal and external stakeholders who took part in our Future Labs. We also thank Andreas Schleicher, Director, and Dirk van Damme, interim Head of CERI, for their comments on the draft, and the CERI Governing Board, which provided encouragement, ideas, and feedback throughout the process. We are grateful for their guidance.

Within the Secretariat, this volume was produced as part of the work on *Trends Shaping Education,* under the leadership of Tracey Burns. Marc Fuster led the analysis of the report, developing the scenarios and drafting Chapters 3, 4 and 5. Tracey Burns authored Chapter 1 and contributed to the analysis and drafting of Chapters 4 and 5. Joshua Polchar authored Chapter 2 and additionally provided helpful comments on the full draft. Simona Petruzzella and Dhiman Talapatra provided the graphics. Sophie Limoges and Leonora Lynch-Stein contributed to the final stages of preparation for publication.

Marc Fuster and Tracey Burns

Table of contents

FIGURES

INFOGRAPHICS

Executive Summary

There are always multiple versions of the future – some are assumptions, others hopes and fears. To prepare, we have to consider not only the changes that appear most probable, but also the ones that we are not expecting. In 2020, the global COVID-19 pandemic has reminded us of how comfortable assumptions about the future may change in an instant.

Back to the future of education: Four OECD Scenarios for Schooling is a tool to support long-term strategic thinking in education. Inspired by the ground-breaking 2001 OECD Schooling for Tomorrow scenarios, these scenarios can help identify potential opportunities and challenges and stress-test against unexpected shocks. We can then use those ideas to help us better prepare and act now.

Why scenarios?

Scenarios are fictional sets of alternative futures. They do not contain predictions or recommendations. Imagining multiple scenarios recognises that there is not only one pathway into the future, but many. **Chapter Two** provides an overview of strategic foresight, highlighting three main benefits: 1) to reveal and test assumptions, 2) stress-test and future-proof plans, and 3) generate shared visions of the future to support action in the present. The chapter sets out key steps for using the scenarios, including questions for identifying implications and taking strategic action.

The four OECD Scenarios for the Future of Schooling

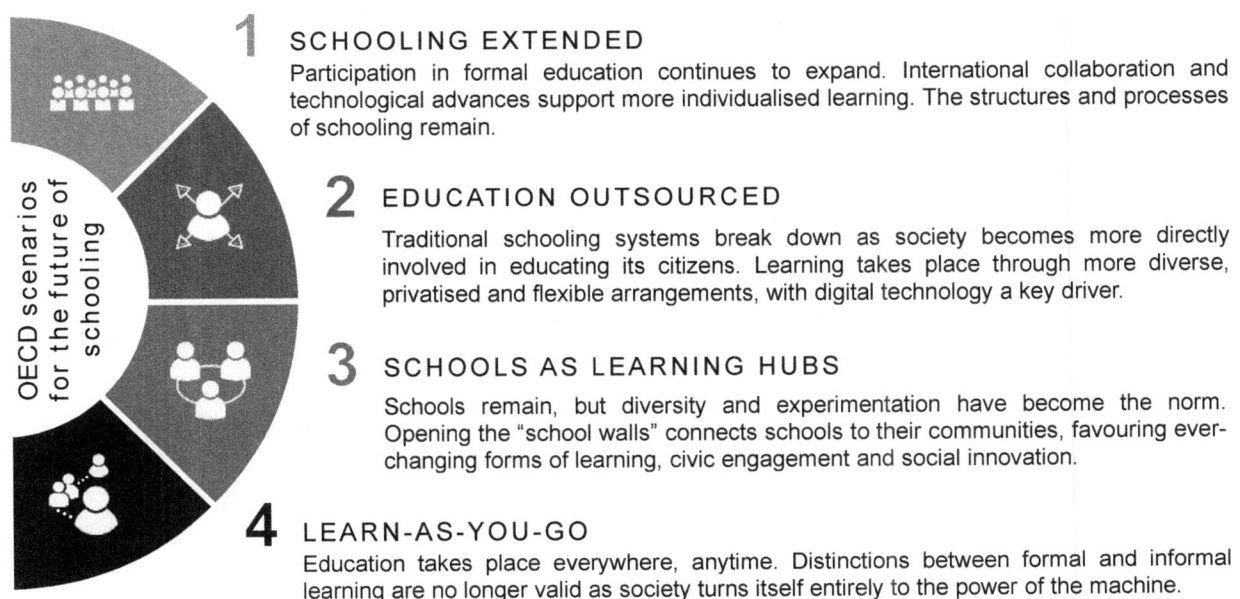

OECD scenarios for the future of schooling

1 SCHOOLING EXTENDED
Participation in formal education continues to expand. International collaboration and technological advances support more individualised learning. The structures and processes of schooling remain.

2 EDUCATION OUTSOURCED
Traditional schooling systems break down as society becomes more directly involved in educating its citizens. Learning takes place through more diverse, privatised and flexible arrangements, with digital technology a key driver.

3 SCHOOLS AS LEARNING HUBS
Schools remain, but diversity and experimentation have become the norm. Opening the "school walls" connects schools to their communities, favouring ever-changing forms of learning, civic engagement and social innovation.

4 LEARN-AS-YOU-GO
Education takes place everywhere, anytime. Distinctions between formal and informal learning are no longer valid as society turns itself entirely to the power of the machine.

Understanding the present helps us think about the future

Chapter Three looks at how education's goals and functions, structures and organisation, and processes and practices have unfolded over the last two decades. It covers the continuing expansion of formal education and our evolving understanding of human learning. It addresses modern shifts in learning objectives and looks at the ways in which education policy and practice works to prepare teachers, schools and systems to effectively respond to such changes.

The four OECD scenarios are presented in **Chapter Four** along with key questions for discussion. The scenarios have a time frame of approximately 20 years – long enough for significant change beyond immediate political cycles, but not too remote for anyone except futurists and visionaries.

What futures for schooling? Seven tensions and paradoxes

Education must evolve to continue to deliver on its mission of supporting individuals to develop as persons, citizens and professionals. In a complex and quickly changing world, this might require the reorganisation of formal and informal learning environments, and reimagining education content and delivery. In an ageing world, these changes apply not just to basic education, but to lifelong learning as well.

But, what is the best way to do this? Just as there is no "one" future, there is no single correct path to the futures of education. And indeed, the future is not a place where problems will magically disappear. By exploring, reflecting and preparing, we can respond to difficult challenges more effectively. **Chapter Five** sets out seven inherent tensions that must be considered in this process:

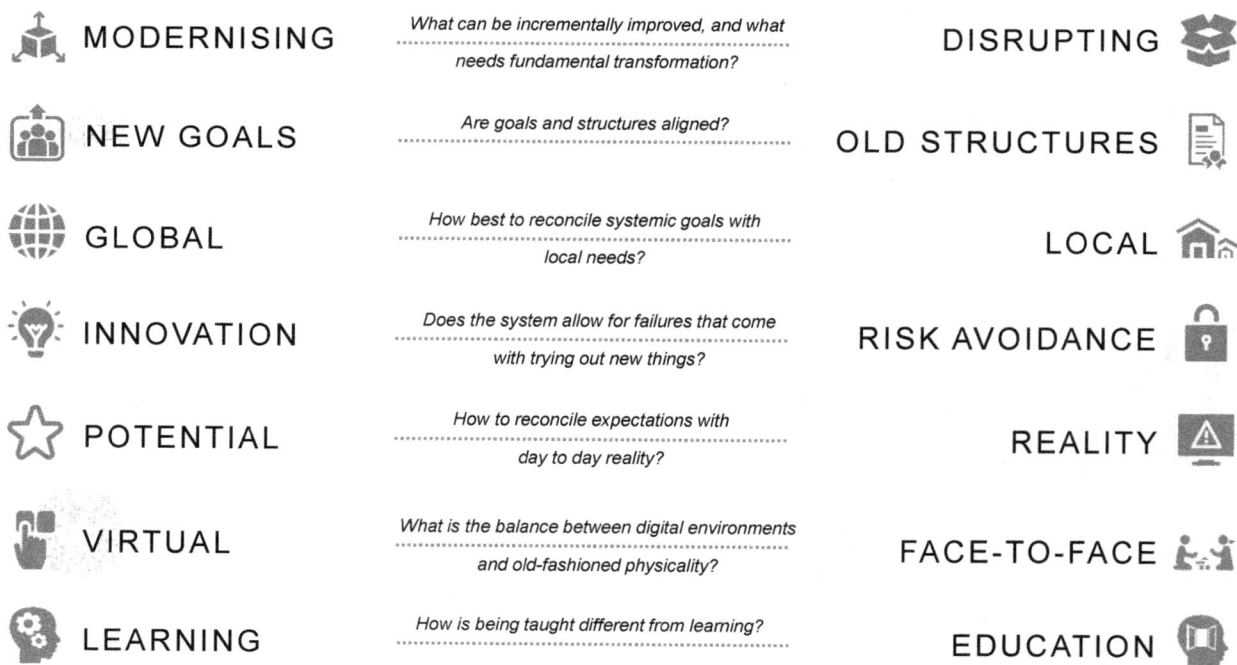

MODERNISING	What can be incrementally improved, and what needs fundamental transformation?	DISRUPTING
NEW GOALS	Are goals and structures aligned?	OLD STRUCTURES
GLOBAL	How best to reconcile systemic goals with local needs?	LOCAL
INNOVATION	Does the system allow for failures that come with trying out new things?	RISK AVOIDANCE
POTENTIAL	How to reconcile expectations with day to day reality?	REALITY
VIRTUAL	What is the balance between digital environments and old-fashioned physicality?	FACE-TO-FACE
LEARNING	How is being taught different from learning?	EDUCATION

A large body of CERI work has focused on the need for education to be better informed by evidence, awareness of what is taking place in other places and at other times, and by the need to consider the bigger, long-term picture. This volume follows proudly in that tradition. In our rapidly changing world, education cannot rely on lessons of the past to prepare for the future. The future is here, and education systems need to learn from it. Our success will depend on how effectively we use our knowledge to anticipate the future, and how quickly we take action to shape it.

1 Back to the future of education: Four OECD scenarios for schooling

Our world is in a perpetual state of change. There are always multiple versions of the future – some are assumptions, others hopes and fears. To prepare, we have to consider not only the changes that appear most probable, but also the ones that we are not expecting. Inspired by the ground-breaking 2001 Schooling for Tomorrow scenarios, this report provides four scenarios for the future of education to 2040, showing not a single path into the future, but many. Using these scenarios can help identify the opportunities and challenges that could be in store for education. We can then use those ideas to help us better prepare and act now.

Education for a changing world

Our world is changing. More people are being born and many of us are living longer. The unprecedented digital transformation of the global economy and society has increased connectivity of economic markets and the ethnic, linguistic and cultural diversity of our societies. These changes are not cosmetic, but rather a fundamental transformation in the balance of economic power and ways in which we live.

Education has been tasked with providing the skills and competencies needed to operate in this modern world. It is a powerful tool to reduce inequity. However, while virtually all children and adolescents in OECD countries participate in primary and lower secondary education, inequality – between countries and between individuals – is increasing, and the gap between rich and poor is at its highest level in 30 years.

Education must evolve to continue to deliver on its mission of supporting individuals to develop as persons, citizens and professionals. It must remain relevant to continue to shape our children's identity and integration into society. In a complex and quickly changing world, this might require the reorganisation of formal and informal learning environments, and reimagining education content and delivery. In an ageing world, these changes are likely to apply not just to basic education, but to lifelong learning as well.

By providing the competencies needed to operate in the modern world, education has the potential to influence the life outcomes of the most disadvantaged. It can help combat the increasing fragmentation and polarisation of our societies, and empower people and communities to take charge of their own civic processes and democratic institutions. Access to learning and knowledge not only opens doors to individual and collective opportunities, it has the potential to reshape the future of our global world.

But… the future is inherently unpredictable, because it is always in the making. Close your eyes and think of something that happened over the last 20 years that you would never have expected. Be it the coronavirus pandemic, the invention and ubiquity of smart phones or something else, the truth is that the future likes to surprise us. This convoluted year 2020 is a reminder of how our comfortable assumptions about the future may change in an instant. Although challenging, this is a call to action, a reminder that we can better prepare for both seen and unforeseen futures if we so choose.

Multiple futures

Traditionally, the year 2020 has held great allure for future thinkers. At the turn of the 20th century, imagining life in the distant time of 2020 generated rich predictions, from everyone living in houses that fly to not needing transport at all, because we can all teleport. Even half-way through that century, predictions for 2020 were something of a fad, and it was not the case that being closer in time made them more accurate:

> "By 2020 we could have well-trained animal employees, including ape chauffeurs." (RAND Corporation Long-Range Forecasting Study, 1968)

Much of our thinking of the future is linear, and based on extending currently existing trends. But trends slow, accelerate, bend and break. Unforeseen events can disrupt even long-standing trends. Opinions differ on historical developments and, even when there is agreement, the future is rarely just a smooth continuation of past patterns. Moreover, we do not know in advance which trends will continue and which will change course, or in what context. Sometimes, we can just be plain wrong.

> "The horse is here to stay but the automobile is only a novelty – a fad."
> (President of Michigan Savings Bank, warning Henry Ford's [inventor of the automobile] lawyer not to invest in the Ford Motor Company, 1903)

In the absence of concrete facts or evidence about the future, the only way to meaningfully understand the future is through dialogue. The future cannot be passively observed. It must be actively discussed in order to learn from it and identify and agree upon actions for today. Imagining multiple scenarios for the future thus recognises that there is not only one pathway into the future, but many (OECD, 2001[1]).

Scenarios are more than just an extrapolation of a given trend, but they can take trends into account by describing how the future might look if one or more trends were to continue (or change course). Scenarios themselves have no intrinsic value; it is the process of creating or using them in the context of strategic dialogue that makes them worthwhile.

The original OECD Schooling for Tomorrow scenarios

In 2001 the OECD/CERI programme "Schooling for Tomorrow" published a set of six futures thinking scenarios. Aimed at sharpening understanding of how schooling might develop in the years to come and the potential role of policy to help shape these futures, the scenarios brought together the "big picture" of strategic goals for education intertwined with the complex and the long-term processes of change. Intentionally fictional, the scenarios did not contain predictions or recommendations. Rather, as with all scenarios, they were constructed for the purpose of learning and taking action in the present. This was achieved by generating, testing, and reframing ideas about what might happen.

At the time, the authors noted that "Perhaps surprisingly, forward thinking... has been relatively little developed in education compared with other policy sectors, despite education's fundamental characteristic of yielding benefits over very long time spans" (OECD, 2001, p. 77[1]). In the almost two decades since, future thinking in education has become more popular but it has tended to coalesce around aspirational visions and roadmaps of desirable futures. These aspirational visions have been used to set agendas and spark dialogue among diverse groups of stakeholders about the curriculum, pedagogy and system delivery that would be needed to make these visions a reality.

Although powerful, by focusing on the delivery of a desired future, those approaches do not prepare systems for unexpected shocks. They do not take into account that the future likes to surprise us. Being future-fit in a challenging and uncertain context requires identifying a number of different plausible future scenarios, exploring what impacts they could have and identifying potential implications for policies. This volume aims to do this, using as its starting point the 2001 Schooling for Tomorrow Scenarios. Connecting to broader futures thinking across policy domains and revisiting and updating the scenarios from almost 20 years ago, this report provides four scenarios for the future(s) of education.

This volume: Four OECD Scenarios for the Future of Schooling

After this introduction, **Chapter Two** provides a brief sketch of strategic foresight methods. It looks at elements of a foresight system and how one might begin to think about using foresight and future thinking methodologies as a way to plan and prepare future-fit systems. Strategic foresight is required whenever there is a high degree of uncertainty surrounding changes to the relevant future context. This applies as much to broad national decisions as to decisions in particular sectors or policy domains such as education.

Two examples from very diverse education systems – Finland and Singapore – are provided to illustrate concretely some of the ways strategic foresight plays out in education.

Chapter Three offers an overview of some of the main trends in education policy and practice in the last decades. It begins with a look at how education has become massified and expanded, reaching more people and increasingly extending throughout the lifespan. It outlines the rising expectations for education and their impacts on multiple areas of schooling and instruction, from evaluation, assessment and certification processes to teaching and teacher polices. The chapter also looks at how education governance has changed and what impacts that has had on our design, delivery and expectations for the future of the sector.

Chapter Four provides a set of four scenarios for the future of schooling to 2040. They have been constructed in a time frame of approximately 20 years – long enough for significant change to occur beyond immediate political cycles, but not so far off as to be too remote for anyone except futurists and visionaries. The alternative futures are a) schooling extended; b) an outsourcing of education and resulting surge of learning markets; c) schools as learning hubs and d) the end of school-based learning and demise of schooling more generally.

The volume ends with **Chapter Five,** which looks at the key implications and tensions that emerge from the scenarios. It explores the policy questions that become visible when imaging these multiple futures. Just as the goals that schools work towards are various and complex, so too are the potential futures that unfold as they are intertwined with the daily reality of the school and its defining processes. The chapter does not provide direct answers; as those emerge in the use and consideration of the scenarios within a specific context. Rather, it highlights those areas that deserve closer attention and where further discussion can be most valuable.

Finally

As the methodologies for educational forward-thinking remain under-developed, there is much to be done in building a "toolbox" of such approaches to inform the policy-making process. Scenarios are one vehicle for doing this. By stimulating dialogue at multiple levels and among key stakeholders, the scenarios come alive with the realities of a particular country or setting. The scenarios are not meant to be understood as polished final statements about the future but the starting point for a process of genuine engagement. This book is meant to challenge, to inspire, to stimulate critical and creative thinking on the multiple futures of education.

A large body of CERI work has been founded on the need for educational decision-making to be better informed by evidence, by awareness of what is taking place in other places and at other times, and by the need to consider the bigger, long-term picture. This volume follows proudly in that tradition.

References

OECD (2001), *What Schools for the Future?*, Schooling for Tomorrow, OECD Publishing, Paris, [1] https://dx.doi.org/10.1787/9789264195004-en.

2 Scenarios: A user guide

Attempting to predict or forecast the future is of limited benefit in a world of high uncertainty. What is highly valuable, however, is to identify a number of different plausible future scenarios, explore what impacts they could have and identify potential implications for policies. Scenarios are sets of alternative futures in the form of snapshots or stories giving an image of a future context. They are intentionally fictional, and never contain predictions or recommendations. Scenarios do not consider what will happen, or what should happen; only what might happen. Participation and dialogue are indispensable to the effective use of scenarios. Through purposing, exploring, identifying implications, and taking strategic action, scenarios help us learn from the future to reframe and reperceive our understanding of the present.

Introduction

The purpose of this chapter is to explain how scenario planning can be used by a variety of audiences, those who want to use ideas about futures that haven't occurred to play their part in shaping the future that will. For those wishing to become practitioners of strategic foresight or to create their own scenarios, please refer to the many resources on this topic.[1]

Why do you need to think about the future?

Education systems currently face multiple pressures, including economic disruption; international tensions; polarisation and declining trust; large-scale migration; and ageing populations. The immediacy of today's challenges often means that governments fail to take the time to step out of the here and now and engage with the future at all (Fuerth and Faber, 2012[1]). At the same time, the future will be no less challenging: climate-related crises, further digitalisation of economies and societies, and new forms of political turbulence both at home and abroad could make for a future that is very different from what is commonly expected.

What does it mean to be future-fit in such a challenging context? Attempting to predict or forecast the future is of limited benefit in a world of high uncertainty. What is highly valuable, however, is to identify a number of different plausible future scenarios, explore what impacts they could have and identify potential implications for policies. It is also important to look beyond the scope of traditional policy silos and consider how multiple developments can intersect and interact in unexpected ways. Change may be happening further and faster than our deliberative (and sometimes lengthy) policy processes are designed to cope with, and when change grows exponentially, so too must an education system's ability to respond to it.

How do you think about the future?

Strategic foresight is a discipline which involves the structured consideration of ideas about the future to identify ways to make better decisions in the present. It is founded on the principle that our ability to predict the future is always limited, but that it is possible to make wise decisions anyway by imagining and using multiple futures. Strategic foresight is required whenever there is a high degree of uncertainty surrounding changes to the relevant future context. This applies as much to broad national decisions as to decisions in particular sectors or policy domains such as education. Strategic foresight has three main benefits:

- *Anticipation*: identifying what's changing and how to prepare for it; avoiding blind spots; considering developments that do not seem intuitively relevant, likely, or impactful, but which could catch us by surprise.
- *Policy innovation*: revealing options for action that make sense in new circumstances, and which reframe or refresh our understanding of the present.
- *Future-proofing*: stress-testing existing plans, strategies, or policies by subjecting them to varying conditions.

The word 'user' occurs frequently in strategic foresight practice. This is because, unlike prediction and forecasting, which attempt to identify one correct future that is the same for everyone, strategic foresight explores multiple versions of the future that help someone in particular. The envisaged user in this publication is the reader's educational establishment or organisation – for example a school, a ministry of education, or a municipality.

Box 2.1. Futures thinking in education: Finland

Skills anticipation and views on the future of schooling

Finland is a fertile land for futures thinking. In both the public and private sectors, megatrends and drivers are identified and scenarios and visions built from national to local level. There is a standing Committee for the Future in the Parliament, each government publishes its Report on the Future and the ministries prepare their own futures reviews. Prime Minister's Office and Sitra, The Finnish Innovation Fund, coordinate a national foresight network that brings together a wide range of actors from different areas of society.

The education sector is no exception to this trend. The world around the school is complex and rapidly changing, and there is a long tradition of using futures thinking to anticipate the content of education and better understand the possibilities and challenges affecting the development of teaching and learning. An example of this is the National Forum for Skills Anticipation, a foresight expert body bringing together hundreds of representatives from working life, education, research and administration to anticipate changes in skills demand. The results of the Forum's work on quantitative and qualitative skills needs and proposals for developing education are currently being explored and debated by various parties.

Another example was the Future of Learning 2030 Barometer, launched in 2009 by the Finnish National Agency for Education (formerly Finnish National Board of Education). Aimed at supporting the reform of the core curricula, the Barometer was repeated several times over successive years.

The Barometer relied on techniques of futures studies, such as the Delphi method. The use of three panels helped to capture the diverse views among different groups and bring these in dialogue with each other. In its second edition, a set of five scenarios was created to further highlight the diverse potential discontinuities the future could hold. Eventually, key issues addressed in the curriculum process had close connections to those highlighted by the Barometer, such as changing roles of teachers and students, crossing boundaries between the society and the school and within the school itself and the importance of transversal competences in teaching and learning.

Sources: Airaksinen, Halinen, and Linturi (2017[2]) and Ministry of Education and Culture (2019[3])

Find out more:

Foresight activities and work on the future, Prime Minister's Office, Finland, https://vnk.fi/en/foresight.

Strategic foresight methods

Strategic foresight uses many different methods such as scanning the horizon for signals for future change[2]; building visions of desirable futures and working out what steps would be needed to realise them; and road mapping the development of technologies. For the purposes of this chapter, two sets of methods are particularly important: trends and scenarios.

Trends are a fundamental part of futures thinking. They show multiple ways in which the past and the present give rise to the future by forecasting what might happen if a trend were to continue. Trends help us to tell the difference between what is constant, what is changing, and what is constantly changing. They also often challenge our assumptions and biases about what is really happening. Publications such as Trends Shaping Education (OECD, 2019[4]) have the additional value of demonstrating the importance of broader developments outside a given domain because the biggest disruptions to a system may well originate outside that system.

> Scenarios are intentionally fictional, and never contain predictions or recommendations. Participation and dialogue are indispensable to the effective use of scenarios.

Scenarios are sets of alternative futures (usually three or four to compare) in the form of snapshots or stories giving an image of a future context. They are intentionally fictional, and never contain predictions or recommendations. They are constructed for the purpose of learning and taking action in the present. This is achieved by generating, testing, and reframing ideas about what might happen.

Scenarios are more than just an extrapolation of a given trend, but they can take trends into account by describing how the future might look if one or more trends were to continue (or change course). Scenarios themselves have no intrinsic value; it is the process of creating or using them in the context of strategic dialogue that makes them worthwhile.

Why do you need scenarios?

Scenarios are particularly widespread in the practice of strategic foresight, and multiple schools of thought exist on how they should be developed and used. In general though, for readers of this publication, scenarios are a particularly beneficial foresight approach because of three aspects:

- *Exploration*: scenarios offer a safe space for experts to disagree and challenge each other's assumptions. Knowing that a scenario is not a future we expect to occur means we can be freer in our discussions. It is not possible or desirable to be 'right' about the future in a scenario discussion. This is partly why scenarios come in sets rather than just as one. Exploring the future allows us to let go of our deeply held assumptions which may be proven unfounded and harmful if left unchallenged.

- *Context*: scenarios encourage us to consider what the future will feel like; what it would be like if the paradigm that governs our way of thinking were to change. Whereas forecasting and predictions tend to focus on individual metrics or events, scenarios allow us to consider the future as a whole: 'the big picture'.

- *Narrative*: scenarios can become powerful tools for creating shared understanding within an organisation on how to act. By creating a set of experiences about the future with their own characters, events, and logic, good scenario narratives are memorable enough to become part of an organisation's way of thinking.

Box 2.2. Futures thinking in education: Singapore

Long-term thinking and planning

The Singapore government started developing foresight capabilities in the late 1980s, beginning with scenario planning at the Ministry of Defence. Scenario planning was subsequently adopted as a tool for long-term policy thinking and development across the public service.

As a foresight think tank in the Strategy Group of the Prime Minister's Office, the Centre for Strategic Futures (CSF) was established in 2009 to strengthen long-term thinking and planning capabilities across the public service by evaluating new methods of futures thinking, identifying black swan events and developing contingency plans, free of the demands of day-to-day operational responsibilities. CSF also builds and maintains a network of foresight practitioners and strategic planners, including various ministry and agency foresight units, futures alumni and international thought leaders.

A key outcome of foresight work is the development of a mind-set and culture of future-orientation across the public service. In the area of education, driving forces such as rapid technological advancements, threat of inequality, and changing youth aspirations have important impact on how we prepare our people for the future. As such, the Ministry of Education (MOE) launched a reform movement in recent years, called "Learn for Life", which comprises six thrusts that have been progressively introduced in recent years:

- "Joy of Learning" that emphasises purposeful learning driven by interest and passion, rather than just academic achievements.
- "One Secondary Education, Many Subject Bands" that allows students to learn different subjects at a pace according to their abilities.
- "Education as an Uplifting Force" that strengthens education as a social leveller, with significant investment in pre-school education and bursary schemes to ensure that everyone can access and afford education.
- "Learning Languages for Life" that supports the learning of Mother Tongue Languages that reflect Singapore's multicultural society and heritage, as well as foreign languages to prepare students to engage with the region and the world.
- "Refreshing Our Curriculum" that enhances character and citizenship education, strengthens digital literacy for all, and helps students get to know Asia; and
- "Skills Future for Educators" that supports educators in nurturing future-ready learners.

As the world remains complex and uncertain, and as Singapore continues to face unique challenges, the disciplined practice of foresight will be ever more critical. CSF will continue to support the public service in deepening its long-term thinking and planning capabilities, so that we can make better decisions today and be better prepared for tomorrow.

Source: Ministry of Education (2020[5])

Find out more:

Centre for Strategic Futures, Strategy group, Prime Minister's Office, Singapore, https://www.csf.gov.sg/.

How do you use scenarios?

1. PURPOSING
Establishing why scenarios are useful

- What is the organisation that is considering its future?
- Why does the organisation exist?
- Who are the actors with which the organisation interacts?
- What strategy or programme or policy is the organisation considering that would benefit from discussion of scenarios?

2. EXPLORING
Understanding the logic and characteristics of the scenario

- What signals are there in the present that they may already be coming true?
- How would someone living in each of these worlds of the future describe it to someone from today?

3. IDENTIFYING IMPLICATIONS
Considering how the user would fare in the scenarios

- What new threats and opportunities emerge for us in each scenario?
- What strengths and weaknesses would our organisation have in each scenario?
- Which of the scenarios are we most and least prepared to survive and thrive in, and why?
- What new strategic challenges and priorities are raised by these scenarios?

4. TAKING STRATEGIC ACTION
Returning to the present-day actions of the user organisation

- What is our strategic inventory?
- How do existing practices perform in each scenario?
- What new changes or signs of change do we need to watch out for?
- What new options are there to combine existing strengths with new opportunities?
- What new options are there to avoid existing weaknesses combining with new threats?
- What new questions do we need to address today?
- What new options for action make sense in light of the discussion?

Box 2.3. Stumbling blocks in scenario-based policy dialogue

Stumbling block #1: Attempting to gauge probability of the scenarios (either in isolation or in comparison to one another). This can also manifest itself in attempts to disregard a scenario because it seems unlikely to occur.

- *Why this occurs*: this often stems from the misconception that scenarios are intended to be forecasts or predictions. Many also assume that only probable future developments are worth discussing.

- *Why it is unhelpful*: attempting to judge probability draws attention to the validity of the scenarios themselves, rather than the strategy they are intended to serve. It is much easier to criticise someone else's work than our own strategy! It also undermines a premise of scenario planning, which is to accept that a good deal of future developments are unpredictable, and many things will occur that seem unlikely from today's perspective. Furthermore, it is possible to learn positive lessons today from fictional future events, even if they never really occur.

- *How to address it*: participants in a dialogue can be reminded of events that have recently occurred that would have seemed almost impossible a decade prior (there are many); it can also help to refer to fables that are known fictions, but which nonetheless contain valuable lessons. Scenarios are fictions about the future from which we can learn. Another useful technique is to ask leading questions about what developments in the present positively suggest that the given scenario is already coming true.

Stumbling block #2: Attempting to identify actions that would neutralise or 'solve' the characteristics of a scenario that seem problematic. This can also occur when participants describe a scenario as 'unstable' and look for ways to return their image of the future to one closer to the status quo or current expectations.

- *Why this occurs*: this happens when participants accept that a scenario could occur, but find it undesirable and believe that they have the capacity to prevent it coming true or reverse it after it does. It is very common in policy dialogues for participants to fail to make a distinction between (A) what policy as a whole is capable of achieving; and (B) what their own organisation can achieve alone and through its actual partnerships.

- *Why it is unhelpful*: a central principle of scenarios is that the user should be forced to consider how they would face alternative futures that they are not in a position to determine. Only through the discipline of understanding one's own limitations can one identify concrete actions that can be taken to succeed in the future. Scenarios may reveal very insightful options for public policy as a whole, but if the dialogue does not reveal actions for the user to take then no impact will come of the exercise.

- *How to address it*: participants should be asked to divorce themselves from the present by imagining what they would do if they fell asleep today and woke up in the world described by the scenario. It can also help to structure participants' thinking using verbal devices, such as insisting that every sentence used to explore a scenario begin with the words "this is a world in which…"

Find out more:

Strategic Foresight, OECD, https://www.oecd.org/strategic-foresight/

References

Airaksinen, T., I. Halinen and H. Linturi (2017), "Futuribles of learning 2030 - Delphi supports the reform of the core curricula in Finland", *European Journal of Futures Research*, Vol. 5/1, http://dx.doi.org/10.1007/s40309-016-0096-y. [2]

Fuerth, L. and E. Faber (2012), *Anticipatory Governance Practical Upgrades: Equipping the Executive Branch to Cope with Increasing Speed and Complexity of Major Challenges*, Institute for National Strategic Studies, Washington, DC. [1]

Ministry of Education (2020), *Learn for Life – Ready for the Future: Refreshing Our Curriculum and Skillsfuture for Educators*, https://www.moe.gov.sg/news/press-releases/learn-for-life--ready-for-the-future--refreshing-our-curriculum-and-skillsfuture-for-educators (accessed on 25 March 2020). [5]

Ministry of Education and Culture (2019), *Anticipation of skills and education needs in Finland*, https://minedu.fi/documents/1410845/4150027/Anticipation+of+skills+and+education+needs/d1a00302-8773-bbe0-39a0-46e0d688d350/Anticipation+of+skills+and+education+needs.pdf. [3]

OECD (2019), *Trends Shaping Education 2019*, OECD Publishing, Paris, https://dx.doi.org/10.1787/trends_edu-2019-en. [4]

Notes

[1] For example, Ramírez, R., and A. Wilkinson (2016), *Strategic Reframing: The Oxford Scenario Planning Approach*, Oxford University Press, Oxford and New York.

[2] Horizon scanning itself can be done in an infinite number of ways, depending on what the user is looking for. This can include iterative reviews, automated text mining, expert surveys, and web scraping. The purpose is not to find the 'right' ideas about the future, but to identify instead the strong and weaker signals of change occurring in the present that could be surprising and significant in the future from the perspective of the user.

3 Taking stock of the present: Trends in education and schooling

Understanding the present helps us think about what the future holds. This chapter looks at how education's goals and functions, structures and organisation, and processes and practices have unfolded over the last two decades. It addresses the continuing expansion of formal education in people's first stages of life, from early education and care through to tertiary education. It explores the evolving notions of human learning and how learning objectives for individuals have changed. It also looks at the ways in which education policy and practice works to prepare teachers, schools and systems to effectively respond to such changes.

Introduction

This report offers a set of scenarios for the future of schooling. In order to think about how the future might unfold, we must take stock of the present. This chapter does this by looking into the main developments and issues in education and schooling over the last two decades. Key trends include the rising participation in formal education; our expanded understanding of human learning; and the growing expectations that society has of schools and teachers and therefore the ways with which education policy and practice prepares teachers, schools and systems to respond to such demands.

A front-end model of education continues to expand

Participation in formal education early in life is not just a given but a major trend that is on the rise. Virtually all children and adolescents in OECD countries participate in formal education through compulsory enrolment in primary and lower secondary education programmes. Furthermore, high enrolment rates often extend beyond compulsory education: for children and adolescents in some OECD countries, full enrolment in education can last for up to 16 or 17 years.

Participation in non-compulsory levels of education is also growing across the board. More than 90% of 4 and 5-year-olds participated in early childhood education in almost all OECD countries in 2017, as did the vast majority of 3-year-olds in 1 out of 3 countries. Participation in education has also kept rising at the other end of compulsory schooling: in just ten years, the OECD average proportion of tertiary-educated young individuals (24-34 years-old) grew from 35 to 44% between 2008 and 2018 (OECD, 2019[1]).

Figure 3.1. An educated future

Population size by level of educational attainment, worldwide, 1970 – 2100

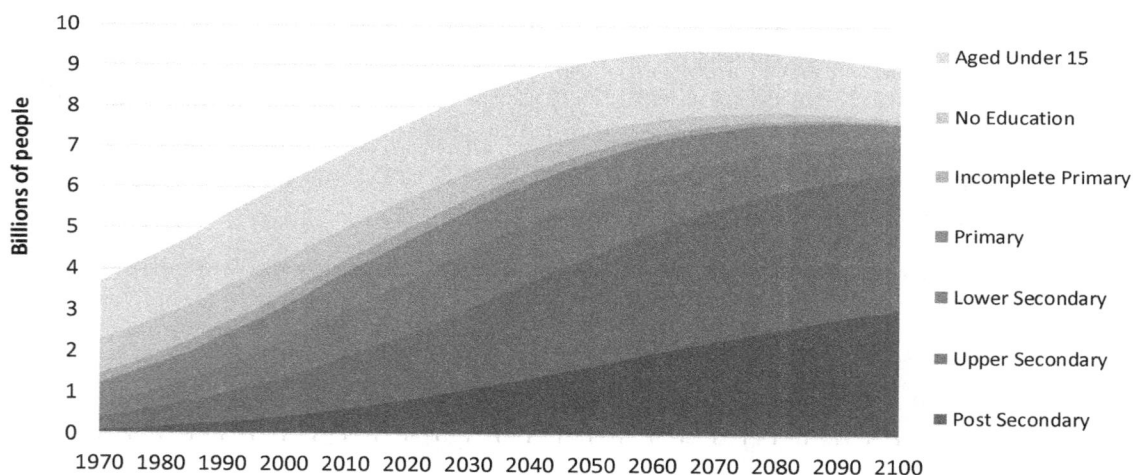

Note: Population projections are based on the Centre of Expertise on Population and Migration (CEPAM) Medium (SSP2) scenario.
Source: Wittgenstein Centre for Demography and Global Human Capital (2018[2]).

Large returns from formal education...

Education functions as a common good, supporting fundamental rights such as civic and political participation and adequate levels of health and well-being (UNESCO, 2015[3]). Highly educated individuals show greater engagement with the democratic process, are more likely to report they have a say in government, to volunteer and to trust others (OECD, 2017[4]). They are also more likely to have better physical and mental health, as higher levels of education are associated with reduced risk-taking behaviour and healthier lifestyles (OECD, 2019[5]; 2019[6]).

In addition, education is critical for the knowledge economy (OECD, 2019[7]). Education builds human capital; it increases individuals' capabilities, enhancing economic productivity and facilitating the development and adoption of frontier technologies (Goldin and Katz, 2007[8]). In such a context, highly educated individuals enjoy a large premium in employability and earnings (OECD, 2019[1]; 2019[6]). Despite clear signs of occupational polarisation (OECD, 2017[9]) – that is, a decline in the share of total employment attributable to middle-pay jobs, which has been offset by increases in the shares of both high- and low-pay jobs – higher skill levels developed through education may still be required of all workers if jobs in the low end of the wage distribution are to involve increasingly complex, non-routine tasks not replaceable by technology (Autor, Levy and Murnane, 2003[10]) such as in care, for instance.

Much has been written about the potential impact of technological advances on the future of work and jobs, with views ranging from future labour and job scarcity to more extreme visions on the end of work (Brown and Keep, 2018[11]). Advances in computers' artificial intelligence, vision and movement capabilities could certainly have a strong impact on tasks carried out by the majority of workers in currently existing jobs (Elliott, 2017[12]). Inferring future workforce implications is however difficult; many economic and organisational factors mediate the application of technology in the economy (Brynjolfsson and Mitchell, 2017[13]) and as computer capabilities evolve so does the demand for skills in labour markets – demand for social and emotional skills, for example, has kept rising over the last four decades (Deming, 2017[14]).

Access to education, even at the earliest stage (OECD, 2017[15]; 2020[16]), can hence continue to yield large benefits later in life. Returns on education increase while opportunities to access learning grow outside of traditional schools and colleges, including education in community colleges, for-profit universities, technical institutes and digital programmes of various forms. Yet, because employers learn about their employees' skills only as tenure in the job increases, many use readily available, albeit imperfect, measures to screen prospective workers, such as academic credentials (Bol, 2015[17]). As a result, educational attainment is still a better predictor of employment than actual skills in many countries (OECD, 2019[6]).

An important question is whether more refined methods for capturing people's skills beyond what is taught at school will become a source of liberation, allowing academic institutions to focus more on learning and less on sorting, freeing up economic resources for both individuals and society. A second order question that emerges from this, and a farther-reaching one, pertains to the value of learning institutions in a society that accepts the ubiquitous and hands-on nature of learning and is capable of better measuring a wide range of its possible outcomes. In such a world, would the raison d'être of schools disappear?

...while barriers to access still exist

Despite the growing value of education and the expansion of schooling, uneven access to education services remains a challenge. This is the case for instance for those students with migrant and refugee status, whose schooling experiences are strongly conditioned by language and cultural barriers, changes in syllabi and teaching methods across countries and schools (OECD, 2017[18]; 2018[19]; Cerna, 2019[20]). It relates to rural education, particularly in more remote and sparsely populated areas, which often have smaller schools with greater limitations in human and financial resources and where students often commute long hours to attend school (OECD, 2017[21]; 2018[22]). It has to do with pupils with learning disabilities, physical impairments and mental disorders, who do not always have access to mainstream educational settings, although this trend is reversing in some systems (OECD, 2017[23]).

In addition, students from disadvantaged socioeconomic background are more likely to struggle at school, have lower participation rates in early childhood education and care (ECEC) and lower expectations of and actual enrolment in tertiary education (OECD, 2019[1]). A key driver of inequality in access and opportunity is the intergenerational transmission of advantage. Advantaged students are more likely to have advantaged parents, both in terms of education and labour force participation, which not only poses moral and political dilemmas but negatively impacts economic productivity and innovation (OECD, 2017[24]).

Levelling the playing field has been an important priority for OECD countries over the last two decades (OECD, 2019[25]). Some policies, such as access to ECEC, funding systems that account for differences in schools' socioeconomic composition, longer school days and greater access to non-formal learning activities can help mitigate social, economic and cultural barriers (OECD, 2017[26]; 2018[22]; 2019[27]). Others, such as grade repetition, early tracking and uncontrolled school choice schemes appear to contribute to reproducing them (OECD, 2019[28]; 2018[29]).

Massive schooling and lifelong learning: Friends or foes?

The population in OECD countries is ageing, largely in good health (OECD, 2019[7]). A growing number of adults continue to work beyond the statutory retirement age and access to learning throughout life becomes an important factor supporting people's professional growth. However, participation of 25-64 year-olds in formal education is strongly linked to participation in the labour market, and tertiary-educated individuals are twice as likely to participate than those with an education below upper-secondary education (OECD, 2019[1]). A number of institutional and circumstantial barriers stand in the way of adults' access to learning opportunities, such as relevance, costs or lack of flexibility (OECD, 2019[30]; 2018[31]).

Yet, not all learning takes place in the context of formalised learning institutions. Aware of this, countries across the globe have set up skills definition frameworks and associated assessments schemes for recognising adults' non-formal and informal learning (Braňka, 2016[32]; Singh, 2015[33]; Werquin, 2010[34]). Digitalisation has only increased the avenues for non-formal and informal learning participation, especially considering that digital engagement has steadily grown across all age groups over the last two decades (OECD, 2019[7]). A wide range of open educational resources (OER), such as massive, open, online courses (MOOCs), now facilitate access to learning opportunities for all, particularly in tertiary education (Orr, Rimini and van Damme, 2015[35]).

At the same time, the informal, largely self-directed nature of these learning opportunities can become a barrier for those lacking the necessary skills and dispositions to engage independently and fruitfully (Littlejohn et al., 2016[36]). How meaningful learning opportunities appear to their potential users is as important as how accessible they are. Early proponents of lifelong learning were aware of this issue when recognising that education "must endeavour to instil, especially in children, a taste for self-learning that will last a lifetime" (Faure et al., 1972, p. 184[37]). However, how good our education systems are in building individuals' lifetime motivation for learning (OECD, 2000[38]) is a relatively unstudied question in comparison to the analysis of short-term academic measures. Education and educational research must increase attention to the kind of skills that enhance engagement with learning in the long run if concerned with lifelong and life-wide learning. Emerging findings in the behavioural sciences and its growing intersection with education may be of particular relevance for this discussion.

In addition, because adult learning tends to be discussed in the framework of labour market needs, questions around meaning and accessibility of learning opportunities for senior citizens have also traditionally been mostly overlooked. Living longer entails changes in the meaning of old age. People now spend an increasing number of years in retirement (OECD, 2019[7]). Seniors' learning needs thus go beyond those related to labour activity, for example in making healthy transitions from work into retirement (Schuller, 2019[39]; Istance, 2015[40]). Importantly, regarding learning as part of an active and healthy ageing should not be at odds with the fact that older, frailer seniors often face situations of dependency, isolation and poor health. Supporting elders' access to learning opportunities should thus recognise the circumstances of the most elderly as well younger seniors (Boudiny, 2013[41]).

Learning for a world in change

Developing a well-trained workforce equipped with advanced competencies is central to remaining competitive in the global knowledge economy. This idea, common in political discourses and policy documents, together with the expectations of more educated and demanding parents, helps explain what can be defined as a global urgency for learning.

Not surprisingly, schools and teachers are in the limelight. They are meant to support academic learning and excellence and their impact is increasingly closely monitored. An example of this is the growing focus that countries have placed on measuring learning outcomes over the last two decades, which in turn generates still greater public and political attention (Verger, Parcerisa and Fontdevila, 2018[42]).

At the same time, the enterprise of education becomes increasingly challenging as changes in the wider environment of schools unfold. Take literacy for example: traditionally the main measure of success of an education system, literacy is no longer about reading and writing only. In a digital world, it also relates to making sense of abundant, often conflicting pieces of information, assessing the reliability of sources and the validity of given claims within concrete cultural contexts (OECD, 2018[43]).

Rising expectations of schooling

Today, education is about the capacity to process information and solve problems, which includes strong disciplinary knowledge as well as analytical, creative and critical thinking skills. It is about broader abilities that, while related to cognition, have also to do with interpersonal and intrapersonal functioning, such as social and emotional skills, tolerance and respect for others as well as capacities to self-regulate and better understand one's own learning processes (Luna Scott, 2015[44]; Pellegrino, 2017[45]).

Arguably, these attributes are not of higher value today than they were in the past. Yet, in the past, only those in leading social roles were expected to develop such abilities. This has all changed in a world where work develops in flatter, dynamic and multicultural structures, a world with growing risks for individuals and where people more actively shape the state of events locally and globally, virtually and face-to-face vis-à-vis traditional powers such as the church, the traditional press or the state (OECD, 2019[7]).

Advanced cognitive and attitudinal competences, once considered beyond the reach of most, are now expected as the norm. Yet, national and international assessments highlight striking differences in learning outcomes, raising concerns around "learning poverty" (World Bank, 2017[46]) and "skills gaps" – although the latter are subject of a heated debate (Modestino, Shoag and Ballance, 2019[47]; Shierholz and Gould, 2018[48]). With rising expectations of schooling, the role of schools in maintaining a balance between equity, an excellent education provision and catering to individual learning needs is as increasingly challenging as it is necessary.

A growing understanding of how people learn

Large-scale schooling appeared as a response to the needs of modern societies, emerging in the 18th and 19th century to equip children with and certify knowledge for the emerging industrial economy. These systems continued to grow, additionally playing the role of taking care of children while parents were at work, increasingly so with the decline in child labour and the entry of women into the labour market during the 20th century. Schools additionally familiarised learners with social roles and rules, religious customs and, increasingly, the secular values of larger and diverse communities of civic and national belonging. Yet, by the time massive schooling emerged, little was known about how learning actually worked. Schools traditionally operated under a "factory model" where standardised processes, rote-learning, memorisation and information recall were the norm – and this is still the case in many places today.

Nowadays, we have a much more robust understanding of human learning (National Academies of Sciences, Engineering, and Medicine, 2018[49]; Cantor et al., 2018[50]; Kuhl et al., 2019[51]; Dumont, Istance and Benavides, 2010[52]). Today, we know that human brains are plastic and that people learn differently, even given similar environments and learning methods. We know that learners are not empty vessels or blank slates. The prior beliefs, experiences and skills that they bring into their learning are central in the processing of new information. Prior knowledge needs thus to be leveraged, and counterbalanced in the case of misconceptions, if learners are to move from fragmented facts and routine processes to recognising how problems relate to what they already know and to develop and apply skills to solve them.

How meaningful the context is to learners and how actively they participate in their own learning are crucial aspects as well. Different experiences offer different learning opportunities. Additionally, research is clear on how close the link is between cognitive and affective, social, and emotional functions. A positive environment supports learning, and so does the possibility for learners to articulate knowledge and engage in conscious reflection on how such knowledge is developed. Articulation and reflection are social in nature: discussion with, and guidance and support from others (teachers, parents, peers) are invaluable learning resources.

Working out change: Lessons from the learning sciences

Various combinations of learners, educators, content and resources can enhance learning in schools (Darling-Hammond et al., 2019[53]). A first consideration is building a learning environment where learning is safe, that fosters warm relationships among its members and is sensitive to cultural and functional diversity (OECD, 2019[54]; 2020[55]; 2010[56]; 2017[23]). Support systems for students, including academic support within and beyond the classroom and the consideration of learners' physical and emotional health, reinforce positive environmental conditions (Burns and Gottschalk, 2019[57]; 2020[58]).

At the level of instruction, motivation is key. Curricula need to identify core competencies while leaving room for educators and students to adapt it to their needs and interests. Important to curriculum design is the recognition that students develop meaningful understanding through prior knowledge transfer, epistemic reasoning and meta-cognitive skills rather than by accumulating facts in an ever-growing variety of topics (Pellegrino, 2017[45]; OECD, forthcoming[59]).

Deep learning processes require teaching strategies featuring cognitive activation, providing space for self- and collaborative reflection and offering well-designed scaffolding, i.e. the instructional technique in which sufficient support is offered when tasks are first introduced to students. It is gradually removed when students start mastering the expected knowledge and skills (Paniagua and Istance, 2018[60]).

In addition, schools must provide learning opportunities to all students (Schmidt et al., 2015[61]; OECD, 2016[62]) and work proactively to develop the habits and mind-sets that favour resilience and positive attitudes towards learning (Chernyshenko, Kankaraš and Drasgow, 2018[63]).

Evaluation and assessment tools need to align with these objectives, which is currently not often the case (OECD, 2013[64]): the pre-eminence of individual testing vis-à-vis collaborative learning, or testing based on information recall within schools that are increasingly digitalised are good examples of such dissonance. 21st century assessments need to look into students' integrated knowledge, skills and attitudes within applied tasks, responding effectively to the increasing need of capturing processes that may manifest validly in multiple ways, such as creativity (Vincent-Lancrin et al., 2019[65]).

Future-fit evaluation needs to adapt to diverse student bodies and hold high expectations for all regardless of social stereotypes (Kuhl et al., 2019[51]; Tarabini, Castejón and Curran, 2020[66]; OECD, 2017[23]). Advanced assessments go beyond what can be memorised to help learners to be more self-aware about who they are and how they learn (Conley, 2018[67]). Greater student ownership over such information can improve assessment formative power for a range of skills, not only those that have been traditionally valued. In turn, soft skills, such as readiness to learn, may be a key for individuals to keep developing themselves, intellectually and professionally, as they grow older (Fernandez and Liu, 2019[68]).

New technologies with learning analytic functions may soon support learners and teachers to do this (Kuhl et al., 2019[51]; Wyatt-Smith, Lingard and Heck, 2019[69]; OECD, 2018[70]), but greater capacity of practitioners and decision-makers to use educational data is required (Schildkamp, 2019[71]) in order for these technologies to work effectively. Even with the investments in this area (OECD, 2019[25]), educational data are still often not used, misused and abused in a number of ways (Burns, Köster and Fuster, 2016[72]).

Teachers, teaching and teacher policies

Despite the importance of modernising education, system-wide change in massive schooling systems has proven to be an elusive task. Central to schooling improvement is the extent to which education systems are able to better leverage its main asset: teachers. Expressed almost two decades ago, however, the following description is still unsettling relevant today:

> The more complex and uncertain the world in which we live, the more that alternative sources of knowledge and influence are available to students, the more open schools become to diverse clienteles, and the more varied the organisational and pedagogical strategies that teachers should deploy, the greater... the levels of professional skill needed to meet them. There are growing expectations that they [teachers] can operate in new organisational structures, in collaboration with colleagues and through networks, and be able to foster individual student learning. These call for demanding concepts of professionalism: the teacher as facilitator and knowledgeable, expert individual and networked team participant, oriented to individual needs and to the broader environment, engaged in teaching and in R&D (OECD, 2001, pp. 71-72[73]).

Developing a high-quality teaching workforce

Improving the quality of the teaching workforce has been high on the policy agenda in recent decades (OECD, 2005[74]; 2019[25]). Countries face challenges around an ageing teaching workforce, high rates of attrition among new teachers or a shortage of quality teachers in disadvantaged schools. Additionally, they may be concerned about the quality of teachers' preparation for the job, which has also a large influence on the attractiveness of the profession (OECD, 2019[75]).

A variety of policy actions can be linked to these priorities. Many countries have reformed teacher salary scales and career structures to ensure options for professional advance and diversification exist and are rewarded (OECD, 2019[76]). Diverse forms of teacher appraisal have been developed and strengthened and teaching standards and competence frameworks have been introduced to inform teacher education and training, certification and career progress (Révai, 2018[77]; OECD, 2013[64]).

Many systems cover teacher shortages by drawing upon keeping teachers in the classrooms later in their lifespans (OECD, 2013[78]). However, as the number of healthier, competent and motivated senior teachers continues to grow, a tension may emerge between safeguarding their right to work and favouring the entry of younger professionals. In turn, such policies may further complicate efforts to address other demographic imbalances, such as ensuring the teacher force is reflective of the student population – in terms of gender or ethnic composition, for example (OECD, 2015[79]; 2017[18]; 2010[56]).

In parallel, improving teacher qualifications, skills and training has been a key policy priority (OECD, 2019[25]). This relates to developing comprehensive teacher education curricula and offering relevant field experience to prospective teachers. It has to do with easing the transition from school to work for novice teachers, providing time for practical experimentation and socialisation with peers, and continuously nurturing professional skills with training, opportunities for reflective practice and on-the-job research (OECD, 2005[74]; 2019[80]; 2019[76]; Paniagua and Sánchez-Martí, 2018[81]).

Nevertheless, outstanding issues remain. Despite wide evidence on the key role that motivations and emotions play in teaching and learning, teacher education as well as entry, selection, certification and hiring criteria in many systems do not give proper consideration to teachers' affective and motivational capacities (OECD, 2019[80]; Guerriero, 2017[82]). In addition, despite efforts to build "sheltered environments" for novice teachers via induction and mentoring programmes, questions exist regarding how accessible and meaningful opportunities for practical experience are in initial teacher preparation (OECD, 2019[76]). Also being considered is how desirable it is to quickly induce early career teachers into schools that may not be open to scrutinising and revising their practices, that is, to innovate (Paniagua and Sánchez-Martí, 2018[81]).

Education systems have also placed a great emphasis on improving teachers' access to continuous professional development: extending training options, securing time and leave entitlements for participation and linking training to career progression (OECD, 2019[76]). However, training in the form of one-time or short-series of externally provided learning is not ideal. Knowledge, that is, "assimilated information and the understanding of how to use it" (Hess and Ostrom, 2007[83]), cannot be 'transferred' like a piece of paper. Evidence use, improvement and innovation go hand in hand: teachers use knowledge available to create new solutions and generate new knowledge throughout the process (Révai, 2020[84]).

Hence, teachers are brokers of their own knowledge, increasingly often by organising themselves in peer networks that extend beyond the "school walls" (Paniagua and Istance, 2018[60]; OECD, 2015[85]). Sharing, exchange, dialogue and collaboration among teachers and within partnerships between these and other actors, such as research institutions, move beyond linear knowledge transmission models to create an innovation-research ecosystem where evidence and new methods can be incorporated effectively by all teachers within their respective contexts (OECD, 2019[76]; Révai, 2020[84]). A better understanding about how these arrangements work is necessary if policy makers are to foster, collaborate with, sustain, enhance and hold such organisational structures accountable (Lima, forthcoming[86]).

Teachers as knowledgeable and networked professionals

Teachers that are more experienced and knowledgeable provide higher quality teaching, which results in better student outcomes. Knowledgeable teachers – with knowledge that is explicit and codified and tacit, implicit, fruit of experience (Révai and Guerriero, 2017[87]) – are better classroom managers, ensuring that students are organised, attentive and focused. They experiment new approaches, providing students with a thought-provoking instruction to keep them engaged in the task. They are attentive and responsive to the emotional needs of pupils, and actively build warm relationships with them (Ulferts, 2019[88]).

Good teachers diagnose a situation and identify learning needs. With a diagnostic, they have to apply one of various potential solutions, a dilemma that they resolve by mobilising knowledge (Révai and Guerriero, 2017[87]; Pollard, 2010[89]). This is knowledge on their subject content, on general pedagogical practices and, increasingly, knowledge on technology. Its acquisition may come directly from the study of evidence and active engagement in research, as well as from professional experience and through peer collaboration and exchange (Guerriero, 2017[82]; Harris, Mishra and Koehler, 2009[90]; OECD, 2019[80]).

Different teaching strategies may support student learning in different ways. For instance, teachers may design activities where students play an active role in directing their own learning, as in project-based learning or by building on play and game mechanics. Other teachers may prefer to engage students via storytelling, suggestive analogies and provocative examples, and open-up topics to discussion. Teachers may often combine various strategies depending on the task, their own skills and confidence and the level of student responsiveness (Paniagua and Istance, 2018[60]).

This offers a perspective in which practitioners actively use, connect and adapt different forms of knowledge to their contexts and practice. This is a complex competence, which involves evaluating specific learning cases and contextual factors, such as students' prior knowledge, attitudes and motivation, curricular goals and available learning resources, and connecting them to knowledge of teaching and learning (Guerriero and Révai, 2017[91]). Such a view of teaching moves away from the perception of teachers as technicians who implement procedures in a curriculum towards one of professionals whose practice is discretionary and builds on knowledge and judgement. In this sense, innovation is at the heart of teachers' professional practice: teachers must constantly develop new solutions and adapt those of others by means of study, intuition and collaboration (Paniagua and Istance, 2018[60]; Révai, 2020[84]).

Evolution of education governance

The distribution of power within education systems has changed substantially in the last four decades. Based on the assumption that officials, governors, managers and professionals who are close to local operations know best what should be done, many education systems have moved towards greater decentralisation, granting local actors more discretionary power in the exercise of their responsibilities. Political reforms and wider global trends such as globalisation and expanded connectivity have shifted power in other directions as well: "upwards, towards international organisations" and "sideways to private institutions and non-governmental organisations" (Theisens, 2016, p. 56[92]). Central governments, still responsible for the outcomes of the schooling system have adapted to new roles, moving away from central planning and control and strengthening accountability and support in relation to local actors.

More flexible and result-oriented systems

Public administration worked traditionally through planning by "breaking down a goal or set of intentions into steps, formalising those steps so that they can be implemented almost automatically, and articulating the anticipated consequences or results of each step" (Mintzberg, 1994, p. 108[93]). With greater local autonomy and vertical, performance-based accountability mechanisms like large-scale assessments, educational administrations exercise a more indirect form of control through goal-setting, evaluation and steering. Furthermore, many systems have adopted market-inspired tools to govern areas such as school management and student enrolment (Sahlberg, 2016[94]), although with disparate results (Waslander, Pater and van der Weide, 2010[95]; Lubienski, 2009[96]).

Central education administrations have strengthened support to local actors, redefining the roles and resources of existing structures, such as inspectorates, increasing communication efforts to clarify policy priorities and actions, and setting up mechanisms to translate and mobilise evidence, knowledge and expertise (OECD, 2007[97]). This has spurred experimentation and innovation, strengthened self-evaluation and improvement capacity in schools and the sharing of good practices. Nevertheless, the reverse has also been observed, where policy implementation flaws occurred following miscommunication and rapidly changing priorities, reform overload and fatigue, and when centrally-developed tools (e.g. data, software) were not used locally (Burns, Köster and Fuster, 2016[72]).

Education systems have become more complex, with a broader diversity of actors and a growing number of governance levels in which decisions are made and implemented. Importantly, local autonomy creates the space for a larger and more diverse range of stakeholders to participate in and shape the policy process – with their engagement, feedback and support but also their resistance (Burns and Köster, 2016[98]).

What has been described so far is only part of the story. Greater local autonomy brings as well increased power for actors to self-organise and collaborate. Networks and partnerships are now common for exchanging ideas and learning and optimisation of service delivery. Formed by individuals or organisations, formal or informal in nature, voluntary or mandated, these are more and more common, such as in school-to-school and teacher professional networks and partnerships between educational services and service providers in other fields, public and private (OECD, 2018[22]; 2019[76]; Burns and Gottschalk, 2019[57]; Révai, 2020[84]).

Figure 3.2. Potential stakeholders in education

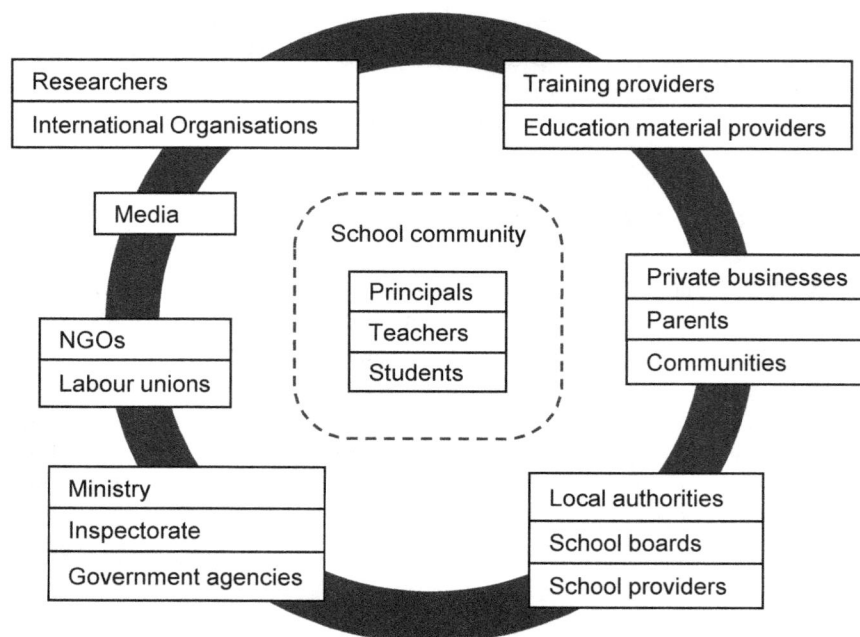

Source: Burns and Köster (2016[98]).

Networks and partnerships may entail a number of undesired outcomes, including increased costs of collaborative activities, lack of capacity, complexity in co-ordination, and diffusion of responsibilities and consequent accountability issues (Lima, forthcoming[86]; Ehren and Perryman, 2017[99]). These need to be taken into account to make sure the costs of partnering do not outweigh its benefits. In addition, a crucial question for governments is how to relate to these networks (Theisens, 2016[92]).

Networks and partnerships imply new ways of thinking, with social actors guided by their own preferences and priorities. Governments need to assess whether and how reactions from stakeholders may favour or hinder advancement towards desired policy objectives or, indeed, whether such goals need to be reformulated, build up jointly outside the administration or defined locally. Once an initiative emerges from communities or local actors (bottom-up), the question for governments becomes *what is next?* The answer varies, and can be different in each particular context: to do nothing, block, facilitate, influence or gain control of such emerging structures (Frankowski et al., 2018[100]).

Building up trust and mobilising legitimacy are key for governing under these complex circumstances, and governments may leverage network structures and alliances to push policies forward (Burns, Köster and Fuster, 2016[72]). Networks and partnerships may be more difficult to manage given the different goals of public and private actors, and the need to effectively coordinate multiple nodes simultaneously. But these may need to be strengthened to make sure education systems leverage external expertise and resources and keep up with rapid changes in the wider environment (Burns and Gottschalk, 2019[57]).

At the same time, establishing these alliances implies dealing with concerns related to quality and equity, such as in potential fragmentation of services provided and unethical behaviour by some of the parties (Verger, 2019[101]). Additionally, because the adoption of policy instruments privileges and nourishes certain actors and particular interests by "determining resource allocations, access to the policy process, and problem representations" (Menon and Sedelmeier, 2010, p. 76; in Verger, Parcerisa and Fontdevila (2018[42]), policy decisions taken in a particular moment in time may have long-term consequences. Potential lock-in effects are aspects of the present that can be crucial to how education's future develop.

Concluding remarks

This chapter has provided an overview of main developments and issues around schooling and formal education provision. It has looked at schooling as a socioeconomic trend, one that has grown for over a century and continues to expand. First, access to formal education continues to increase with the expansion of early learning, a wide range of learning programmes outside of schools and the growth of post-secondary programmes. Second, participation in schooling has also expanded where equity gaps are bridged, both in terms of learning participation and the recognition and accommodation of existing social diversity within learning programmes.

Better insights from the learning sciences hold the promise for eventually being able to deliver on the intention of education reform. Meanwhile, expectations for schooling keep growing. Despite greater access to formal learning, there are persistent and significant learning deficits in large parts of the population, which causes scepticism over both the quality and equity of education provision in current systems. Concerns also exist regarding the provision and nature of lifelong learning. Despite ongoing refinement of learning metrics, artificial distinctions between what is learnt within and out of schools remain too often unchallenged.

Are massive schooling systems fit for purpose? Will their current strengths and challenges be reduced or amplified in a world of increasing complexity? How will they evolve in a more resilient, self-organising society? Should we embrace some sort of technological solutionism? Furthermore, would technological solutions solve schooling shortcomings or could they potentially replace schooling systems entirely? Our current version of schooling systems emerged with the industrial society and whether they will continue to persist remains an open question.

References

Autor, D., F. Levy and R. Murnane (2003), "The Skill Content of Recent Technological Change: An Empirical Exploration", *The Quarterly Journal of Economics*, Vol. 118/4, pp. 1279-1333, http://dx.doi.org/10.1162/003355303322552801. [10]

Bol, T. (2015), "Has education become more positional? Educational expansion and labour market outcomes, 1985–2007", *Acta Sociologica*, Vol. 58/2, pp. 105-120, http://dx.doi.org/10.1177/0001699315570918. [17]

Boudiny, K. (2013), "'Active ageing': from empty rhetoric to effective policy tool", *Ageing and Society*, Vol. 33/6, pp. 1077-1098, http://dx.doi.org/10.1017/s0144686x1200030x. [41]

Braňka, J. (2016), *Understanding the potential impact of skills recognition systems on labour markets: Research report*, International Labour Office, Geneva, https://www.ilo.org/wcmsp5/groups/public/---ed_emp/---ifp_skills/documents/publication/wcms_532417.pdf. [32]

Brown, P. and E. Keep (2018), "Rethinking the race between education and technology", *Issues in Science and Technology*, Vol. 35/1, pp. 31-39, https://issues.org/rethinking-the-race-between-education-technology/. [11]

Brynjolfsson, E. and T. Mitchell (2017), "What can machine learning do? Workforce implications", *Science*, Vol. 358/6370, pp. 1530-1534, http://dx.doi.org/10.1126/science.aap8062. [13]

Burns, T. and F. Gottschalk (eds.) (2020), *21st Century Children, Technology and Physical Health*, OECD Publishing, Paris. [58]

Burns, T. and F. Gottschalk (eds.) (2019), *Educating 21st Century Children: Emotional Well-being in the Digital Age*, Educational Research and Innovation, OECD Publishing, Paris, https://dx.doi.org/10.1787/b7f33425-en. [57]

Burns, T. and F. Köster (eds.) (2016), *Governing Education in a Complex World*, Educational Research and Innovation, OECD Publishing, Paris, https://dx.doi.org/10.1787/9789264255364-en. [98]

Burns, T., F. Köster and M. Fuster (2016), *Education Governance in Action: Lessons from Case Studies*, Educational Research and Innovation, OECD Publishing, Paris, https://dx.doi.org/10.1787/9789264262829-en. [72]

Cantor, P. et al. (2018), "Malleability, plasticity, and individuality: How children learn and develop in context1", *Applied Developmental Science*, Vol. 23/4, pp. 307-337, http://dx.doi.org/10.1080/10888691.2017.1398649. [50]

Cerna, L. (2019), "Refugee education: Integration models and practices in OECD countries", *OECD Education Working Papers*, No. 203, OECD Publishing, Paris, https://dx.doi.org/10.1787/a3251a00-en. [20]

Chernyshenko, O., M. Kankaraš and F. Drasgow (2018), "Social and emotional skills for student success and well-being: Conceptual framework for the OECD study on social and emotional skills", *OECD Education Working Papers*, No. 173, OECD Publishing, Paris, https://dx.doi.org/10.1787/db1d8e59-en. [63]

Conley, D. (2018), *The Promise and Practice of Next Generation Assessment*, Harvard Education Press, Cambridge. [67]

Darling-Hammond, L. et al. (2019), "Implications for educational practice of the science of learning and development", *Applied Developmental Science*, pp. 1-44, http://dx.doi.org/10.1080/10888691.2018.1537791. [53]

Deming, D. (2017), "The growing importance of social skills in the labor market", *Quarterly Journal of Economics*, Vol. 132/4, pp. 1593-1640, http://dx.doi.org/10.1093/qje/qjx022. [14]

Dumont, H., D. Istance and F. Benavides (eds.) (2010), *The Nature of Learning: Using Research to Inspire Practice*, Educational Research and Innovation, OECD Publishing, Paris, https://dx.doi.org/10.1787/9789264086487-en. [52]

Ehren, M. and J. Perryman (2017), "Accountability of school networks", *Educational Management Administration & Leadership*, Vol. 46/6, pp. 942-959, http://dx.doi.org/10.1177/1741143217717272. [99]

Elliott, S. (2017), *Computers and the Future of Skill Demand*, Educational Research and Innovation, OECD Publishing, Paris, https://dx.doi.org/10.1787/9789264284395-en. [12]

Faure, E. et al. (1972), *Learning to be: The world of education today and tomorrow*, International Commission on the Development of Education, UNESCO, https://unesdoc.unesco.org/ark:/48223/pf0000001801 (accessed on 14 November 2019). [37]

Fernandez, F. and H. Liu (2019), "Examining relationships between soft skills and occupational outcomes among U.S. adults with—and without—university degrees", *Journal of Education and Work*, Vol. 32/8, pp. 650-664, http://dx.doi.org/10.1080/13639080.2019.1697802. [68]

Frankowski, A. et al. (2018), "Dilemmas of central governance and distributed autonomy in education", *OECD Education Working Papers*, No. 189, OECD Publishing, Paris, https://dx.doi.org/10.1787/060260bf-en. [100]

Goldin, C. and L. Katz (2007), *The Race between Education and Technology: The Evolution of U.S. Educational Wage Differentials, 1890 to 2005*, National Bureau of Economic Research, Cambridge, MA, http://dx.doi.org/10.3386/w12984. [8]

Guerriero, S. (ed.) (2017), *Pedagogical Knowledge and the Changing Nature of the Teaching Profession*, Educational Research and Innovation, OECD Publishing, Paris, https://dx.doi.org/10.1787/9789264270695-en. [82]

Guerriero, S. and N. Révai (2017), "Knowledge-based teaching and the evolution of a profession", in *Pedagogical Knowledge and the Changing Nature of the Teaching Profession*, OECD Publishing, Paris, https://dx.doi.org/10.1787/9789264270695-13-en. [91]

Harris, J., P. Mishra and M. Koehler (2009), "Teachers' Technological Pedagogical Content Knowledge and Learning Activity Types", *Journal of Research on Technology in Education*, Vol. 41/4, pp. 393-416, http://dx.doi.org/10.1080/15391523.2009.10782536. [90]

Hess, C. and E. Ostrom (eds.) (2007), *Understanding Knowledge as a Commons - From Theory to Practice*, Massachusetts Institute of Technology, Cambridge, Massachusetts; London, England, http://mitpress.mit.edu (accessed on 1 July 2019). [83]

Istance, D. (2015), "Learning in Retirement and Old Age: an agenda for the 21stcentury", *European Journal of Education*, Vol. 50/2, pp. 225-238, http://dx.doi.org/10.1111/ejed.12120. [40]

Kuhl, P. et al. (2019), *Developing Minds in the Digital Age: Towards a Science of Learning for 21st Century Education*, Educational Research and Innovation, OECD Publishing, Paris, https://dx.doi.org/10.1787/562a8659-en. [51]

Lima, G. (forthcoming), "Effectiveness of collaboration networks in education Benefits, challenges and governance", *Education Working Papers*, OECD publishing, Paris. [86]

Littlejohn, A. et al. (2016), "Learning in MOOCs: Motivations and self-regulated learning in MOOCs", *The Internet and Higher Education*, Vol. 29, pp. 40-48, http://dx.doi.org/10.1016/j.iheduc.2015.12.003. [36]

Lubienski, C. (2009), "Do Quasi-markets Foster Innovation in Education?: A Comparative Perspective", *OECD Education Working Papers*, No. 25, OECD Publishing, Paris, https://dx.doi.org/10.1787/221583463325. [96]

Luna Scott, C. (2015), "The futures of learning 2: What kind of learning for the 21st century?", *Education Research and Foresight Working Papers Series* 14, https://unesdoc.unesco.org/ark:/48223/pf0000242996/PDF/242996eng.pdf.multi. [44]

Mintzberg, H. (1994), "The fall and rise of strategic planning", *Harvard Business Review*, Vol. 72/1, pp. 107-114, https://hbr.org/1994/01/the-fall-and-rise-of-strategic-planning. [93]

Modestino, A., D. Shoag and J. Ballance (2019), "Upskilling: do employers demand greater skill when workers are plentiful?", *Review of Economics and Statistics*, pp. 1-46. [47]

National Academies of Sciences, Engineering, and Medicine (2018), *How People Learn II*, National Academies Press, Washington, D.C., http://dx.doi.org/10.17226/24783. [49]

OECD (2020), "Crime & punishment", *Trends Shaping Education Spotlights*, No. 19, OECD Publishing, Paris, https://dx.doi.org/10.1787/945692bd-en.   [55]

OECD (2020), *Early Learning and Child Well-being: A Study of Five-year-Olds in England, Estonia, and the United States*, OECD Publishing, Paris, https://dx.doi.org/10.1787/3990407f-en.   [16]

OECD (2019), *A Flying Start: Improving Initial Teacher Preparation Systems*, OECD Publishing, Paris, https://dx.doi.org/10.1787/cf74e549-en.   [80]

OECD (2019), "A healthy mind in a healthy body", *Trends Shaping Education Spotlights*, No. 17, OECD Publishing, Paris, https://dx.doi.org/10.1787/eb25b810-en.   [5]

OECD (2019), *Balancing School Choice and Equity: An International Perspective Based on Pisa*, PISA, OECD Publishing, Paris, https://dx.doi.org/10.1787/2592c974-en.   [28]

OECD (2019), *Education at a Glance 2019: OECD Indicators*, OECD Publishing, Paris, https://dx.doi.org/10.1787/f8d7880d-en.   [1]

OECD (2019), *Education Policy Outlook 2019: Working Together to Help Students Achieve their Potential*, OECD Publishing, Paris, https://dx.doi.org/10.1787/2b8ad56e-en.   [25]

OECD (2019), *Getting Skills Right: Future-Ready Adult Learning Systems*, Getting Skills Right, OECD Publishing, Paris, https://dx.doi.org/10.1787/9789264311756-en.   [30]

OECD (2019), *PISA 2018 Results (Volume III): What School Life Means for Students' Lives*, PISA, OECD Publishing, Paris, https://dx.doi.org/10.1787/acd78851-en.   [54]

OECD (2019), "Play!", *Trends Shaping Education Spotlights*, No. 18, OECD Publishing, Paris, https://dx.doi.org/10.1787/a4115284-en.   [27]

OECD (2019), *Skills Matter: Additional Results from the Survey of Adult Skills*, OECD Skills Studies, OECD Publishing, Paris, https://dx.doi.org/10.1787/1f029d8f-en.   [6]

OECD (2019), *TALIS 2018 Results (Volume I): Teachers and School Leaders as Lifelong Learners*, TALIS, OECD Publishing, Paris, https://dx.doi.org/10.1787/1d0bc92a-en.   [75]

OECD (2019), *Trends Shaping Education 2019*, OECD Publishing, Paris, https://dx.doi.org/10.1787/trends_edu-2019-en.   [7]

OECD (2019), *Working and Learning Together: Rethinking Human Resource Policies for Schools*, OECD Reviews of School Resources, OECD Publishing, Paris, https://dx.doi.org/10.1787/b7aaf050-en.   [76]

OECD (2018), "A brave new world: Technology and education", *Trends Shaping Education Spotlights*, No. 15, OECD Publishing, Paris, https://dx.doi.org/10.1787/9b181d3c-en.   [70]

OECD (2018), *Equity in Education: Breaking Down Barriers to Social Mobility*, PISA, OECD Publishing, Paris, https://dx.doi.org/10.1787/9789264073234-en.   [29]

OECD (2018), *Responsive School Systems: Connecting Facilities, Sectors and Programmes for Student Success*, OECD Reviews of School Resources, OECD Publishing, Paris, https://dx.doi.org/10.1787/9789264306707-en.   [22]

OECD (2018), *Skills on the Move: Migrants in the Survey of Adult Skills*, OECD Skills Studies, OECD Publishing, Paris, https://dx.doi.org/10.1787/9789264307353-en. [31]

OECD (2018), *The Resilience of Students with an Immigrant Background: Factors that Shape Well-being*, OECD Reviews of Migrant Education, OECD Publishing, Paris, https://dx.doi.org/10.1787/9789264292093-en. [19]

OECD (2018), "Writing in a changing world", *Trends Shaping Education Spotlights*, No. 16, OECD Publishing, Paris, https://dx.doi.org/10.1787/c70a7cb3-en. [43]

OECD (2017), "Citizens with a say", *Trends Shaping Education Spotlights*, No. 13, OECD Publishing, Paris, https://dx.doi.org/10.1787/3092726b-en. [4]

OECD (2017), "Country roads: Education and rural life", *Trends Shaping Education Spotlights*, No. 9, OECD Publishing, Paris, https://dx.doi.org/10.1787/ea43a39d-en. [21]

OECD (2017), "Mind the gap: Inequity in education", *Trends Shaping Education Spotlights*, No. 8, OECD Publishing, Paris, https://dx.doi.org/10.1787/5775ac71-en. [24]

OECD (2017), "Neurodiversity in education", *Trends Shaping Education Spotlights*, No. 12, OECD Publishing, Paris, https://dx.doi.org/10.1787/23198750-en. [23]

OECD (2017), *OECD Employment Outlook 2017*, OECD Publishing, Paris, https://dx.doi.org/10.1787/empl_outlook-2017-en. [9]

OECD (2017), "People on the move", *Trends Shaping Education Spotlights*, No. 11, OECD Publishing, Paris, https://dx.doi.org/10.1787/b3d31c5b-en. [18]

OECD (2017), *Starting Strong 2017: Key OECD Indicators on Early Childhood Education and Care*, Starting Strong, OECD Publishing, Paris, https://dx.doi.org/10.1787/9789264276116-en. [15]

OECD (2017), *The Funding of School Education: Connecting Resources and Learning*, OECD Reviews of School Resources, OECD Publishing, Paris, https://dx.doi.org/10.1787/9789264276147-en. [26]

OECD (2016), *Equations and Inequalities: Making Mathematics Accessible to All*, PISA, OECD Publishing, Paris, https://dx.doi.org/10.1787/9789264258495-en. [62]

OECD (2015), "Gender equality", *Trends Shaping Education Spotlights*, No. 7, OECD Publishing, Paris, https://dx.doi.org/10.1787/ea1ec35f-en. [79]

OECD (2015), *Schooling Redesigned: Towards Innovative Learning Systems*, Educational Research and Innovation, OECD Publishing, Paris, https://dx.doi.org/10.1787/9789264245914-en. [85]

OECD (2013), "Ageing societies", *Trends Shaping Education Spotlights*, No. 1, OECD Publishing, Paris, http://www.oecd.org/education/ceri/Ageing_Societies_Spotlight.pdf. [78]

OECD (2013), *Synergies for Better Learning: An International Perspective on Evaluation and Assessment*, OECD Reviews of Evaluation and Assessment in Education, OECD Publishing, Paris, https://dx.doi.org/10.1787/9789264190658-en. [64]

OECD (2010), *Educating Teachers for Diversity: Meeting the Challenge*, Educational Research and Innovation, OECD Publishing, Paris, https://dx.doi.org/10.1787/9789264079731-en. [56]

OECD (2007), *Evidence in Education: Linking Research and Policy*, OECD Publishing, Paris, https://dx.doi.org/10.1787/9789264033672-en. [97]

OECD (2005), *Teachers Matter: Attracting, Developing and Retaining Effective Teachers*, Education and Training Policy, OECD Publishing, Paris, https://dx.doi.org/10.1787/9789264018044-en. [74]

OECD (2001), *What Schools for the Future?*, Schooling for Tomorrow, OECD Publishing, Paris, https://dx.doi.org/10.1787/9789264195004-en. [73]

OECD (2000), *Motivating Students for Lifelong Learning*, OECD Publishing, Paris, https://dx.doi.org/10.1787/9789264181830-en. [38]

OECD (forthcoming), *OECD Future of Education and Skills 2030: Curriculum Analysis*, OECD Publishing, Paris. [59]

Orr, D., M. Rimini and D. van Damme (2015), *Open Educational Resources: A Catalyst for Innovation*, Educational Research and Innovation, OECD Publishing, Paris, https://dx.doi.org/10.1787/9789264247543-en. [35]

Paniagua, A. and D. Istance (2018), *Teachers as Designers of Learning Environments: The Importance of Innovative Pedagogies*, Educational Research and Innovation, OECD Publishing, Paris, https://dx.doi.org/10.1787/9789264085374-en. [60]

Paniagua, A. and A. Sánchez-Martí (2018), "Early Career Teachers: Pioneers Triggering Innovation or Compliant Professionals?", *OECD Education Working Papers*, No. 190, OECD Publishing, Paris, https://dx.doi.org/10.1787/4a7043f9-en. [81]

Pellegrino, J. (2017), "Teaching, learning and assessing 21st century skills", in *Pedagogical Knowledge and the Changing Nature of the Teaching Profession*, OECD Publishing, Paris, https://dx.doi.org/10.1787/9789264270695-12-en. [45]

Pollard, A. (2010), *Professionalism and pedagogy: A contemporary opportunity: A Commentary by TLRP and GTCE*, TLRP, London, http://reflectiveteaching.co.uk/media/profandped.pdf (accessed on 27 January 2020). [89]

Révai, N. (2020), "What difference do networks make to teachers' knowledge?: Literature review and case descriptions", *OECD Education Working Papers*, No. 215, OECD Publishing, Paris, https://dx.doi.org/10.1787/75f11091-en. [84]

Révai, N. (2018), "What difference do standards make to educating teachers?: A review with case studies on Australia, Estonia and Singapore", *OECD Education Working Papers*, No. 174, OECD Publishing, Paris, https://dx.doi.org/10.1787/f1cb24d5-en. [77]

Révai, N. and S. Guerriero (2017), "Knowledge dynamics in the teaching profession", in *Pedagogical Knowledge and the Changing Nature of the Teaching Profession*, OECD Publishing, Paris, https://dx.doi.org/10.1787/9789264270695-4-en. [87]

Sahlberg, P. (2016), "The Global Educational Reform Movement and Its Impact on Schooling", in *The Handbook of Global Education Policy*, John Wiley & Sons, Ltd, Chichester, UK, http://dx.doi.org/10.1002/9781118468005.ch7. [94]

Schildkamp, K. (2019), "Data-based decision-making for school improvement: Research insights and gaps", *Educational Research*, Vol. 61/3, pp. 257-273, http://dx.doi.org/10.1080/00131881.2019.1625716. [71]

Schmidt, W. et al. (2015), "The Role of Schooling in Perpetuating Educational Inequality", *Educational Researcher*, Vol. 44/7, pp. 371-386, http://dx.doi.org/10.3102/0013189x15603982. [61]

Schuller, T. (2019), *Leadership, Learning and Demographics: The Changing Shape of the Lifecourse and its Implications for Education*, The Further Education Trust for Leadership, https://fetl.org.uk/publications/leadership-learning-and-demographics-the-changing-shape-of-the-lifecourse-and-its-implications-for-education/ (accessed on 10 March 2020). [39]

Shierholz, H. and E. Gould (2018), *Why is real wage growth anemic? It's not because of a skills shortage*, https://www.epi.org/blog/why-is-real-wage-growth-anemic-its-not-because-of-a-skills-shortage/ (accessed on 6 March 2020). [48]

Singh, M. (2015), *Global Perspectives on Recognising Non-formal and Informal Learning*, Springer International Publishing, Cham, http://dx.doi.org/10.1007/978-3-319-15278-3. [33]

Tarabini, A., A. Castejón and M. Curran (2020), "Capacidades, hábitos y carácter: atribuciones docentes sobre el alumnado de Bachillerato y Formación Profesional", *Papers. Revista de Sociologia*, Vol. 1/1, p. 1, http://dx.doi.org/10.5565/rev/papers.2778. [66]

Theisens, H. (2016), "Hierarchies, networks and improvisation in education governance", in *Governing Education in a Complex World*, OECD Publishing, Paris, https://dx.doi.org/10.1787/9789264255364-5-en. [92]

Ulferts, H. (2019), "The relevance of general pedagogical knowledge for successful teaching: Systematic review and meta-analysis of the international evidence from primary to tertiary education", *OECD Education Working Papers*, No. 212, OECD Publishing, Paris, https://dx.doi.org/10.1787/ede8feb6-en. [88]

UNESCO (2015), *Rethinking Education: Towards a Global Common Good?*, United Nations Educational, Scientific, and Cultural Organisation, https://unesdoc.unesco.org/ark:/48223/pf0000232555. [3]

Verger, A. (2019), "Partnering with non-governmental organizations in public education: contributions to an ongoing debate", *Journal of Educational Administration*, Vol. 57/4, pp. 426-430, http://dx.doi.org/10.1108/jea-07-2019-224. [101]

Verger, A., L. Parcerisa and C. Fontdevila (2018), "The growth and spread of large-scale assessments and test-based accountabilities: a political sociology of global education reforms", *Educational Review*, Vol. 71/1, pp. 5-30, http://dx.doi.org/10.1080/00131911.2019.1522045. [42]

Vincent-Lancrin, S. et al. (2019), *Fostering Students' Creativity and Critical Thinking: What it Means in School*, Educational Research and Innovation, OECD Publishing, Paris, https://dx.doi.org/10.1787/62212c37-en. [65]

Waslander, S., C. Pater and M. van der Weide (2010), "Markets in Education: An Analytical Review of Empirical Research on Market Mechanisms in Education", *OECD Education Working Papers*, No. 52, OECD Publishing, Paris, https://dx.doi.org/10.1787/5km4pskmkr27-en. [95]

Werquin, P. (2010), *Recognising Non-Formal and Informal Learning: Outcomes, Policies and Practices*, OECD Publishing, Paris, https://dx.doi.org/10.1787/9789264063853-en. [34]

Wittgenstein Centre for Demography and Global Human Capital (2018), *Wittgenstein Centre Data Explorer Version 2.0 (Beta)*, http://www.wittgensteincentre.org/dataexplorer. [2]

World Bank (2017), *World Development Report 2018: Learning to Realize Education's Promise*, The World Bank, http://dx.doi.org/10.1596/978-1-4648-1096-1. [46]

Wyatt-Smith, C., B. Lingard and E. Heck (2019), "Digital learning assessments and big data: Implications for teacher professionalism", *Education, Research and Foresight Working Papers*, No. 25, UNESCO, Paris, https://unesdoc.unesco.org/ark:/48223/pf0000370940. [69]

4 The OECD Scenarios for the Future of Schooling

This chapter provides a set of four scenarios for the Future of Schooling. Consolidating the original 2001 OECD Schooling for Tomorrow scenarios from six to four, the scenarios consider four alternative futures for 2040:

- **Schooling extended**: an intensification of the current front-end, massive schooling model
- **Education outsourced**: an outsourcing of schooling and resulting surge of learning markets
- **Schools as learning hubs**: a re-purposing of schooling and transformation of schools
- **Learn-as-you-go**: the end of school-based learning and demise of schooling.

Introduction

In 2001, the OECD published *What Schools for the Future?* (OECD, 2001[1]), a set of scenarios on the future of schooling and education. The report remains a thought-provoking contribution to future thinking in education and indeed, almost twenty years later, many of the key issues are still debated today.

However, much has also changed in our world since the turn of the 21st century, both within education and in the wider world. This chapter presents an updated set of scenarios, drawing on the original thinking as well as over a decade of CERI work on Trends Shaping Education.

Although tempting to imagine scenarios as possible recipes for the future from which we can choose a preferred option, it is important to recognise that scenarios are not predictions. As highlighted earlier in this volume, much of our thinking of the future is linear, and based on extending currently existing trends. But trends slow, accelerate, bend and break. Unforeseen events can disrupt even long-standing trends.

Scenarios are designed to foster reflection on the possible ways in which the future may differ from our current expectations. These reflections can then be used to gauge our preparedness for the different possible futures, if they were to happen. Imagining multiple scenarios for the future thus recognises that there is not only one pathway into the future, but many (OECD, 2001[1]).

The original 2001 OECD scenarios presented six possible futures framed and structured along a set of themes: attitudes, expectations, and political support; goals and functions; organisation and structures; the geo-political dimension, and; the teacher force. These were in turn clustered around three axes:

- **The status quo extrapolated**
  - Scenario 1: Robust bureaucratic systems
  - Scenario 2: Extending the market model
- **Re-schooling**
  - Scenario 3: Schools as core social centres
  - Scenario 4: Schools as learning organisations
- **De-schooling**
  - Scenario 5: Learner networks and the network society
  - Scenario 6: Teacher exodus – the meltdown scenario

Looking ahead: Four OECD Scenarios for the Future of Schooling

This update presents four scenarios. They build on and reframe the ideas of re-schooling and de-schooling present in the original set – the expansion of learning markets, the growing investment and role of digital technologies in connecting people as well as its impact on the personalisation of learning.

The scenarios also connect to the ongoing discussion of how to better leverage individual motivation for learning, and recognise and take advantage of its informal and non-formal sources. Technological advances have been interwoven throughout, as have the major changes and trends in education itself (see Chapter 3).

The four OECD Scenarios for the Future of Schooling are presented in Figure 4.1. They have been constructed in a time frame of approximately 20 years, to 2040. This timeframe is chosen as it is long enough for significant change to occur beyond immediate political cycles, but not so far off as to be too remote for anyone except futurists and visionaries.

Infographic 4.1. Overview: Four OECD Scenarios for the Future of Schooling

OECD Scenarios for the Future of Schooling	Goals and functions	Organisation and structures	The teaching workforce	Governance and geopolitics	Challenges for public authorities
Scenario 1 **Schooling extended**	Schools are key actors in socialisation, qualification, care and credentialing.	Educational monopolies retain all traditional functions of schooling systems.	Teachers in monopolies, with potential new economies of scale and division of tasks.	Strong role for traditional administration and emphasis on international collaboration.	Accommodating diversity and ensuring quality across a common system. Potential trade-off between consensus and innovation.
Scenario 2 **Education outsourced**	Fragmentation of demand with self-reliant "clients" looking for flexible services.	Diversification of structures: multiple organisational forms available to individuals.	Diversity of roles and status operating within and outside of schools.	Schooling systems as players in a wider (local, national, global) education market.	Supporting access and quality, fixing "market failures". Competing with other providers and ensuring information flows.
Scenario 3 **Schools as learning hubs**	Flexible schooling arrangements permit greater personalisation and community involvement.	Schools as hubs function to organise multiple configurations of local-global resources.	Professional teachers as nodes of wider networks of flexible expertise.	Strong focus on local decisions. Self-organising units in diverse partnerships.	Diverse interests and power dynamics; potential conflict between local and systemic goals. Large variation in local capacity.
Scenario 4 **Learn-as-you-go**	Traditional goals and functions of schooling are overwritten by technology.	Dismantling of schooling as a social institution.	Open market of "prosumers" with a central role for communities of practice (local, national, global).	(Global) governance of data and digital technologies becomes key.	Potential for high interventionism (state, corporate) impacts democratic control and individual rights. Risk of high social fragmentation.

BACK TO THE FUTURE OF EDUCATION: FOUR OECD SCENARIOS FOR SCHOOLING © OECD 2020

Using the scenarios

Since scenarios are "just stories", they can be entertained and discussed more openly than actual policy choices. Working with scenarios is useful for reflecting on the scenarios themselves as well as in the intervening processes of change, both in terms of broader social developments and potential reactions to them from the education sector.

As a tool to navigate plausible futures, scenarios can be used to:

- Observe how our education systems are evolving.
- Assess potential drivers behind these developments and explore signals in the present that could make these patterns continue as they are, speed up or change course entirely.
- Situate ourselves in these futures and assess how well prepared we are for (whether for expected futures or unexpected changes shock the system – see Box 4.1).

Box 4.1. How well are education systems prepared for uncertainty?

Despite the best laid plans, the future is inherently unpredictable. This message was brought home forcefully in 2020, as countries scrambled to respond to the COVID-19 pandemic.

Two dimensions must be considered when preparing for the future: a) plausibility and b) impact. While certain developments may be more probable than others, we must also prepare for events that are unlikely but highly disruptive if they take place.

In addition to global pandemic, other shocks could include (OECD, 2019[2]):

- natural disasters (highly plausible; impact depends on severity, duration, and experience in preparing for and mitigating the event)
- economic shock/crisis (increasingly plausible in an interconnected global world; impact depends on severity and duration of the shock)
- (cyber) war (plausibility depending on context; impact likely high depending on type of warfare)
- Internet disrupted / communications cut through severing undersea cables or targeting satellites (less plausible, but extremely high impact, particularly if it coincides (accidentally or intentionally) with one of the other shocks)
- human/machine interfaces / General Artificial Intelligence (plausibility and impact still unknown).

The rest of this chapter sets out the four scenarios in detail. Some of the questions to be considered when working with scenarios include (see Chapter 2 for more, including links to additional resources):

- What new changes or signs of change do we need to watch out for?
- What is our strategic inventory (funding something, banning something, promoting a new practice, forming a partnership, etc.)?
- How do existing practices perform in each scenario?
- What new options are there to combine existing strengths with new opportunities, or to avoid existing weaknesses combining with new threats?
- What new options for action make sense today in light of the discussion?

In this chapter, each scenario is additionally accompanied by a set of potential drivers and signals from the present, as well as more concrete questions for discussion. The questions are designed to inspire, challenge, and invite further reflection and discussion by the user.

Scenario 1: Schooling extended

> Participation in formal education continues to expand. International collaboration and technological advances support more individualised learning, yet the structures and processes of schooling remain.

In this scenario, **participation in formal education during the early years of life continues to expand** for most individuals. There is widespread recognition of education as a foundation of economic competitiveness and most countries have intensified efforts to universalise access to formal learning from the first years of life and through past tertiary education. **Formal certificates continue to be the main passports to economic and social success**. At the same time, they are also increasingly insufficient and individuals accumulate alternative credentials and a broad range of volunteering and non-formal work experience – aided by public and private sponsoring in some jurisdictions – to become more attractive for the labour market.

The bureaucratic character of school systems continues. Much **attention focuses on the curriculum**, with many countries operating a common curriculum and assessment tools. Pressure towards uniformity and enforcing standards remains, although greater choice is granted to students in choosing the content of their learning as long as defined core competencies are achieved. With a strong focus on knowledge and skills, values and attitudes are more prominent (e.g. co-operation, entrepreneurship).

Strong international public-private collaboration powers digital learning systems, which are fed with learning resources and data mutualised across countries. Governmental education authorities remain the main locus of decision-making, but their influence has diminished as international providers gain in power. Innovations perceived as successful from the private sector percolate quickly into national systems.

In schools, **the organisation of instruction and student-teacher relations remains generally impervious to change, although there is room for innovation**. Schools continue to operate under a classroom/individual adult model but schedules are more flexible with the adoption of blended instructional methods and rigid boundaries between traditional academic subjects have softened. Continuous analysis of instructional dynamics and evaluating student effort and discipline are possible with learning analytics and facial recognition technology. Feedback to students, teachers and parents is instantaneous, reporting student progress and warnings of misbehaviour. It is no longer necessary to stop-and-test; rather, assessment and instruction take place simultaneously.

Schools and their networks can use economies of scale to more effectively plan and deploy resources by leveraging digitalisation and data information systems. More **marked division of tasks and greater diversification of professional profiles in schools** has emerged. A reduced but distinct, well-trained teaching corps remains in charge of designing learning content and activities, which may be then implemented and monitored by educational robots along with other staff employed under diverse working arrangements (voluntary/paid, part-time/full-time, face-to-face or online), or directly by educational software. New roles, such as learning data analysts, grow strongly, employed in school networks or "learning industries" elsewhere.

As digitalisation allows students to work more autonomously, school staff can focus more intensely on **supporting learners' emotional needs and motivation for learning**. An emphasis on digital tools impacts traditional teaching, and many tasks for educators in the classroom may become restricted to "contingency management". Adapting professional development and career structures to the new situation is critical in this scenario: professionals in schools could feel less satisfied with their job if they perceive a disconnect between their professional development and the tasks they are asked to perform.

Infographic 4.2. Scenario 1: Schooling extended

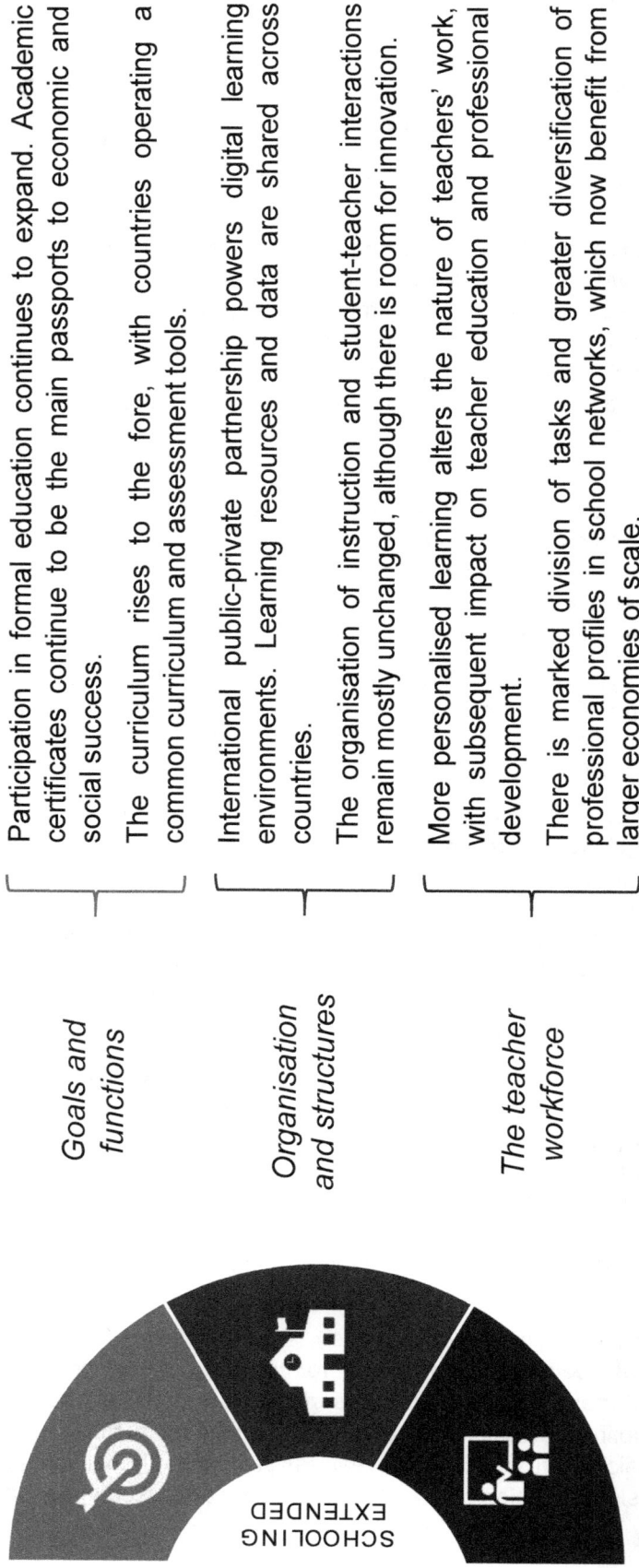

Goals and functions

Participation in formal education continues to expand. Academic certificates continue to be the main passports to economic and social success.

The curriculum rises to the fore, with countries operating a common curriculum and assessment tools.

Organisation and structures

International public-private partnership powers digital learning environments. Learning resources and data are shared across countries.

The organisation of instruction and student-teacher interactions remain mostly unchanged, although there is room for innovation.

The teacher workforce

More personalised learning alters the nature of teachers' work, with subsequent impact on teacher education and professional development.

There is marked division of tasks and greater diversification of professional profiles in school networks, which now benefit from larger economies of scale.

SCHOOLING EXTENDED

Governance and geopolitics

- Strong role for traditional public administrations.
- Increased emphasis on partnerships and international collaboration.

Challenges for public authorities

- Accommodating different demands and ensuring quality across the system.
- Building consensus takes time and may limit innovation.

Box 4.2. Using the scenarios: Schooling extended

Signals from the present and questions for discussion

Many current signs point towards the continuation of massive schooling systems. Some are economic and practical: schools take care of young children, allowing parents to have both work and family life. Some are cultural: In increasingly diverse societies, schools act as a social fabric, building relationships, bridging inequalities and reproducing social norms.

- The current lack of change is often attributed to conservatism and inertia in the system. But in the next 20 years, can we imagine that formal education would be considered as less important? What are the main factors behind the persistence of the massive schooling model? Who are the actors supporting it? Vested interests?

- Another signal from the present is the continuing reliance on traditional forms of educational attainment by employers (e.g. degrees, reputation of tertiary education and training institutions). Why are these traditional measures so impervious to change? Are the attitudes of employers (and students and parents) likely to alter?

- The massification and extension of schooling suggests that lifelong learning will also eventually become part of the system. What is the best way to ensure its quality, and that it can reach those who need it most? Should lifelong learning be a right?

Assuming the continuation of trends in globalisation, multilateralism and international co-operation, closer links between the public sector and private players will increasingly include international partnerships.

- School systems are traditionally based on national models and identities. As schooling becomes increasingly digitalised, could an international school system emerge? Alternatively, could students enrol in a public school system of a country different than their own?

- Should countries join efforts to develop common assessment and instruction tools? What are the pros and cons of such an idea?

- Given the speed of technological change, the most effective protection against cyber risks often comes from the private sector. Are education systems able to partner with these actors in mutually beneficial ways? Which factors could hinder or facilitate this process?

Although this scenario is an extension of the status quo, it could play out in multiple ways. One important variable is investment in education R&D, which has been steadily rising over recent years, mainly pushed by investment in China and the United States. Rapid development of virtual and augmented reality, robotics, blockchain and, increasingly, artificial intelligence, may transform many of the systemic elements that make up the "status quo" as we know it.

- If technology permits teaching to move away from facts and figures, does this mean that teachers will focus more on social and emotional skills? Building stronger relationships with families? What would this mean for teacher education and professional development?

- What would the effects of massive digitalisation of schools be in terms of deployment and distribution of human resources? Professional relationships and collaboration? What about impacts on teachers' professional judgement and accountability?

- Should all educational data be shared with all stakeholders (e.g. students, parents, media) no matter the circumstance? What impacts would this have for student-teacher, teacher-parent and other relationships in schools?

Scenario 2: Education outsourced

> Traditional schooling systems break down as society becomes more directly involved in educating its citizens. Learning takes place through more diverse, privatised and flexible arrangements, with digital technology a key driver.

In this scenario, **diverse forms of private and community-based initiatives emerge as an alternative to schooling**. Highly flexible working arrangements have allowed greater parental involvement in children's education, and public systems struggle with families' pressure towards privatisation. Choice plays a key role – of those buying educational services and of those, such as employers, giving market value to different learning routes.

Great experimentation in organisational forms takes place, including a mix of home-schooling, tutoring, online learning and community-based teaching and learning. In some countries, public and private providers compete to improve the quality of provision. In others, public provision remains purely a "remedial solution", providing parents with free or low-cost child care service and offering children access to learning opportunities and activities to structure their day.

A substantial **reduction of traditional bureaucratic patterns of governance and accountability** takes place as education outsourcing deepens. Different credentials and indicators of quality emerge with the explosion of providers in the "learning market", although private solutions are dependent on how well they meet perceived needs. In addition, governments, in the best interest of children, may retain the power to benchmark and steer market operators through baseline assessments. With greater privatisation and individualised educational paths, concerns about growing social fragmentation have become a recurrent issue in politics across countries and a revival of conscription – in this case with civic rather than military purposes – is becoming a common policy response.

Parents of younger children, rely on public care services or participate in self-organised community networks or market-based services brokered by digital platforms for their care. As learners grow older and more autonomous, and their learning involves more sophisticated tasks, **specialised learning platforms and advice services** (digital and face-to-face, public and private) play a larger role. **Employers become more involved** in the business of education, including large corporations but also small and medium sized enterprises. Traditionally lacking the financial and technical capacity to become involved, SMEs have benefited from increasing financial support derived from the additional resources available from school consolidation processes.

The abandonment of rigid structures of traditional schooling (i.e. year groupings, educational stages) provides learners with greater flexibility to move at their own pace and potentially combine formal learning with other activities. In this sense, greater choice in learning programmes (length, scope, cost, etc.) translates into **learning solutions that are more adaptive to individual needs** and, potentially, more aligned to the goal of lifelong learning. On the other hand, a larger variety of learning suppliers may not result in radically different teaching and learning experiences for learners. **Cultural aspects of traditional schooling organisation may well survive in this scenario**, such as teacher and student roles.

Learning networks bring different human resources together according to perceived needs and as a result traditional conventions, contractual arrangements, and career structures in teaching are rapidly eroded. **There is greater variety of teaching profiles, working arrangements, and professional and reputational status** in a workforce operating in public schooling (physically or digitally), as independent carers, career advisors, skills market analysts, pedagogy specialists in private platforms or others.

Infographic 4.3. Scenario 2: Education outsourced

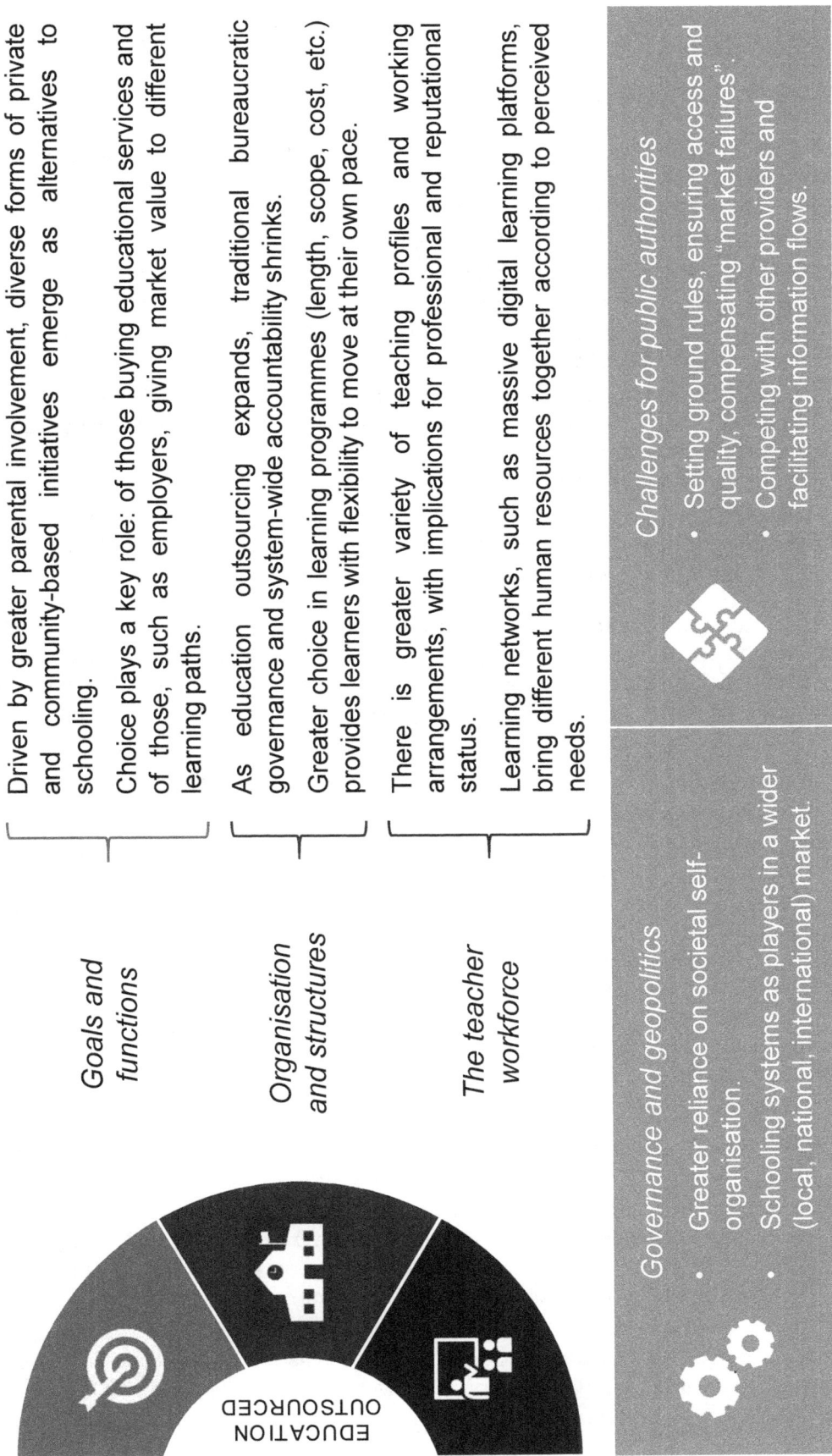

EDUCATION OUTSOURCED

Goals and functions

Driven by greater parental involvement, diverse forms of private and community-based initiatives emerge as alternatives to schooling.

Choice plays a key role: of those buying educational services and of those, such as employers, giving market value to different learning paths.

Organisation and structures

As education outsourcing expands, traditional bureaucratic governance and system-wide accountability shrinks.

Greater choice in learning programmes (length, scope, cost, etc.) provides learners with flexibility to move at their own pace.

The teacher workforce

There is greater variety of teaching profiles and working arrangements, with implications for professional and reputational status.

Learning networks, such as massive digital learning platforms, bring different human resources together according to perceived needs.

Governance and geopolitics

- Greater reliance on societal self-organisation.
- Schooling systems as players in a wider (local, national, international) market.

Challenges for public authorities

- Setting ground rules, ensuring access and quality, compensating "market failures".
- Competing with other providers and facilitating information flows.

Box 4.3. Using the scenarios: Education outsourced

Signals from the present and questions for discussion

There are numerous signals from the present that this scenario could be emerging. New forms of work due to changes in individual preferences, innovations in business models and policy choices lead to increasing experimentation in working arrangements. As digitalisation continues and societies continue to devote greater attention to well-being, we may continue to see alternative work forms and reduced schedules in the years to come (Skidelsky, 2019[3]).

- Would on-demand schooling continue to fulfil the basic social functions that schools are supposed to deliver today? What would the effect of much more flexible schooling arrangements be on children's socialisation?

- A world with reduced work schedules could mean more time for adults to become more involved in children's learning. Conversely, lines between personal and professional could continue to blur, and reduce time for play and informal interaction. Does education have a role in setting boundaries for time spent studying? Can play be a required part of formal education?

- It is often said that schooling should prepare people "for life". If individuals were to spend less time working, should formal education include instruction on leisure? Would this be restricted only to those of school age?

Similarly, increasingly educated parents are already driving more access to diverse public and private solutions for the organisation of teaching and learning. These empowered actors could take matters into their own hands and opt out of the traditional system, with potentially more communitarian approaches to parenting and new ways of ensuring care.

- Would learning "consumers" drive the development of diverse educational products and services or, instead, concentrate around a narrow set of socially agreed "good" options?

- If this scenario were to materialise, could public education provision resemble primary health care services (like visiting the General Practitioner, students go to school for "more serious" interventions)? Would expert human tutoring be a privilege restricted to a few?

- If wealthier families were to opt out of the public system, what would that mean for the resource base for financing public schools? Could advantaged actors be required to contribute directly to schools in poorer neighbourhoods, for example? What about supporting communitarian approaches (school-based or not) in less advantaged areas?

In this scenario, access to information at the touch of a screen allows for teaching and learning without the need of a traditionally qualified teacher. Freed from the classroom, learning is now embedded throughout the lifespan and throughout the day for all citizens.

- Will access to infinite information remove the need for qualified teachers? If not, what aspects of teaching would remain? Are these aspects currently valued in teacher policies?

- Would dynamic learning markets underserve the needs of certain students (e.g. the least advantaged, those without parents to advocate on their behalf)? How conducive this scenario would be in finding ways to support learning and access to work for students with special education needs? What would be the pros and cons?

- Greater choice in learning sources do not necessarily translate into access and use. Should some form of lifelong learning be compulsory, such as with mandatory civic conscription? If yes, would restricting conscription to young adults be a form of discrimination?

Scenario 3: Schools as learning hubs

Schools remain, but diversity and experimentation are the norm. Opening the "school walls" connects schools to their communities, favouring ever-changing forms of learning, civic engagement and social innovation.

In this scenario, strong **schools retain most of their functions**. They continue to look after children and hold activities that structure young people's time, contributing to their cognitive, social, and emotional development. At the same time, **more sophisticated and diverse forms of competence recognition in the labour market** liberate education and thus schools from excessive pressures of credentialism, potentially reversing current trends towards longer individual school careers.

In this scenario, international awareness and exchange is strong, but power shifts to the decentralised elements in the system. **Local actors come up with their own initiatives to achieve the values they consider important**. Schools are defined as strong where intense connections with the community and other local services are developed. This implies that, on the one hand, **systems are no longer based on uniformity**, although strong pressures for corrective action surface where there is evidence that a particular school is under-performing. The criteria upon which schools are judged varies across communities and high-stakes decisions, such as closures, may depend on whether a degree of consensus is achieved among local stakeholders. On the other hand, regulatory and strategic frameworks (local, national, international) and targeted, pre-distributive investment and technical assistance support the action of local communities, and play a key role within communities with weaker social infrastructure.

Schooling is characterised by its comprehensiveness and is grounded in cultures of experimentation and diversity. Personalised pathways are strengthened within a general framework of collaborative work, self-evaluation and peer accountability. Sorting practices such as grades and tracking have been abandoned and **permutations in the organisation of teaching and learning are flexible and constantly changing**. A wide range of sources of learning are recognised and valued and distinctions between formal and non-formal learning become blurred. Learning is ongoing; it is an all-day activity guided by education professionals, but may not always take place within the confines of classrooms and schools.

School activities are planned and designed in the context of broader education planning beyond their own walls, resulting in flexible structures (physical infrastructure, schedules) to accommodate blended learning activities supported by digital information systems. Schools are in this sense the centrepiece of wider, dynamically evolving local education ecosystems, mapping learning opportunities across an interconnected network of educational spaces. This way, **diverse individual and institutional players offer a variety of skills and expertise that can be brought in to support student learning**.

Learning builds on "teachable moments" as defined by collective and learner-specific needs and local developments instead of uniform and rigid curricula. Teachers act as engineers of ever-evolving learning activities, and trust in teacher professionalism is high. **Teachers with strong pedagogical knowledge and close connections to multiple networks** are crucial. This scenario is thus driven by a strong emphasis on teacher initial education and professional development, although these may develop in more flexible and collegiate ways than they do today.

Simultaneously, **schools are open to the participation of non-teaching professionals in teaching**. A prominent role for professionals other than teachers, community actors, parents, and others is expected, and indeed, welcomed. Strong partnerships are also welcomed as schools seek to leverage the resources of external institutions, such as museums, libraries, residential centres, technological hubs and others.

Infographic 4.4. Scenario 3: Schools as learning hubs

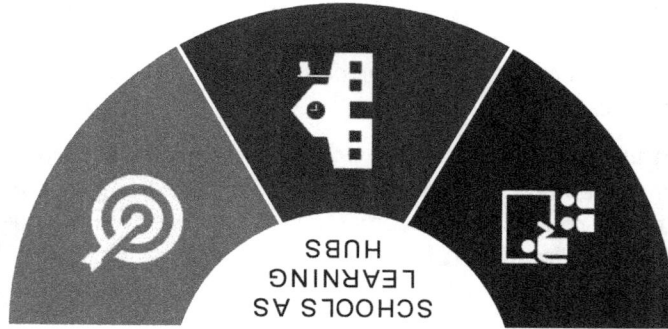

SCHOOLS AS LEARNING HUBS

Goals and functions

Schools retain most of their functions, but new forms of competence recognition systems liberate them from pressures of credentialism.

Systems are no longer based on uniformity: Local actors develop their own initiatives to realise the values they consider important.

Organisation and structures

Experimentation and diversity of pedagogies are the norm. Personalised pathways are strengthened within a framework of collaborative work.

Activities are planned in the context of broader learning ecosystems, mapping opportunities across an interconnected network of educational spaces.

The teacher workforce

Knowledgeable, networked teachers coexist with diverse individual and institutional players offering a variety of skills and expertise.

Strong partnerships leverage the resources of external institutions, such as museums, libraries, residential centres, technological hubs and more.

Governance and geopolitics

- Strong focus on decision making at the local level.
- Self-organising units in diverse partnerships.

Challenges for public authorities

- Diverse interests and power dynamics.
- Tensions between local and system-wide goals.
- Extensive inequality in local capacity.

BACK TO THE FUTURE OF EDUCATION: FOUR OECD SCENARIOS FOR SCHOOLING © OECD 2020

Box 4.4. Using the scenarios: Schools as learning hubs

Signals from the present and questions for discussion

We are already seeing an erosion of formal education credentials (e.g. graduation certificates, degrees) as signals of competence. Several global corporations are already hiring individuals with relevant experience and skill sets but without advanced qualifications (Milord, 2019[4]).

- How likely is it that formal academic credentials would disappear in your systems in the next 15-20 years? In university? Secondary school? What about primary school?

- Would outsourcing sorting and certification functions actually be a source of liberation for schools, in the sense that they no longer have to try and prepare students for the labour market? Or could it be rather a first step towards dismantling the schooling system if other sources of learning become equally (or more) "legitimate"?

- With skills being separated from traditional certification, will more flexible learning choices for students follow? Could distinctions between general and vocational tracks fade away, as students increasingly combine elements of each for their own learning path?

Increasing polarisation and fragmentation in society has prompted calls for building bridges and strengthening belonging in communities. Reinforcing links between schools and local communities is thus aimed at both enhancing learning and reinforcing social capital.

- What forms of collaboration would emerge in (local – global) learning ecosystems? In which ways would adults other than teachers participate? Would teachers be deployed to compensate in those communities where other adults were not available or willing to step in?

- What is the role of formal and informal education in reducing solitude and social isolation? Should schools more actively promote intergenerational exchange as a way to promote social cohesion? Would multi-grade classrooms (currently typical of small rural schools) become more common in a schools as learning hubs future? Could they also include older learners?

- Diverse forms of youth mentorship programmes, such as Big Brothers Big Sisters, are common across OECD countries. Could they be a model to inspire new and diverse institutionalised relationships between and within schools and communities?

Attempts to alter the dynamics and relationships in schooling have long been present. Multiple examples exist of more purpose-oriented, horizontal, collaborative and iterative ways of teaching and learning (e.g. service-learning, citizen science, and more recently Agile methodologies emerging from the 'high tech' sector (Loewus, 2017[5])).

- This scenario assumes that systems have been transformed enough to let go of traditional governance mechanisms such as vertical (grade repetition) and horizontal (early tracking, ability grouping) stratification. Is this realistic in your context?

- Situated learning allows for taking advantage of teachable moments and grounding learning in the here and now. But "unsituated" learning is a very valuable learning source as well, and not only in schools (e.g. TED talks). How can one find the right balance between "instruction" and "exploration"?

- What does this scenario imply for numbers of highly educated teachers, and the kind of teacher education required? Could teachers be the game changers that drive the transformation of systems considered conservative and bureaucratic? If not, what/who else could?

Scenario 4: Learn-as-you-go

> Education takes place everywhere, anytime. Distinctions between formal and informal learning are no longer valid as society turns itself entirely to the power of the machine.

This scenario builds on the rapid advancements of artificial intelligence, virtual and augmented reality and the Internet of Things. Vast connectivity powered by an extensive and rich digital infrastructure and abundance of data have completely changed our perception of education and learning. Learning opportunities are widely available for "free", marking the **decline of established curriculum structures and dismantling of the school system**.

Digitalisation has made it possible to assess and certify knowledge, skills and attitudes in a deep and practically instantaneous manner, and **the intermediary role of trusted third parties** (e.g. educational institutions, private learning providers) **in certification is no longer necessary**. As the distinction between formal and informal learning disappears, massive public resources previously devoted to large-scale schooling infrastructure become liberated to serve other purposes or education through other means.

This scenario sketches a world where all sources of learning become "legitimate" and **people's education advances by leveraging collective intelligence to solve real-life problems**. Lifelong AI personal assistants connect to the environment and among themselves to feed their information systems and propose personalised learning solutions, building on individuals' curiosity and needs, helping to identify knowledge and skills gaps, encouraging creativity and self-expression and connecting learners one another in communities of common purpose. No language barriers exist in access to learning and collaboration with others; accurate translation is now automatic and in real time.

Distinctions between education, work and leisure become blurred. Enterprises make use of AI applications for their recruitment processes, and available workers also obtain information on and access opportunities as well as to continue learning as they work. Part of the old school system infrastructure may remain, although its function is much more open and flexible. There are no mandatory requirements, at least in-person and with fixed schedules. Places for learning welcome children in a drop in basis, as do open and private, digital or face-to-face learning communities.

Similar to scenario 2, alternative "childcare" arrangements may be necessary with the demise of physical schools. In this scenario, digitalisation and "smart" infrastructure favour the creation of safe and learning-rich public and private spaces. Building on surveillance systems, digitally connected, interactive infrastructure, such as intelligent playgrounds, can now look after children while proposing them with learning activities and fostering behaviours towards the satisfaction of certain goals (e.g. healthy lifestyles).

It is difficult to advance the **role of governments vis-à-vis private interests in the market and civil society**. Global digital corporations may play a key role, for instance, in powering learning systems and new human-machine interfaces, but it is also possible that these co-habit with a diversity of bottom-up, non-for-profit initiatives. Although not a given, these developments could develop within the confines of strong regulatory regimes – ensuring algorithm transparency and ethics by design, for example – or through platforms sponsored or directly run by public authorities – local, national or international. Developments around data ownership, democracy and citizen empowerment will have an important impact on these discussions (see the OECD Going Digital scenarios (OECD, 2018, p. 21[6])).

The teaching professional has vanished in this society where rich learning opportunities are available anytime and everywhere and individuals have become prosumers (professional consumers) of their own learning. At the same time, classes, lectures and various forms of tutoring may be commonplace both offline and on, some articulated by humans, others created by the machine.

Infographic 4.5. Scenario 4: Learn-as-you-go

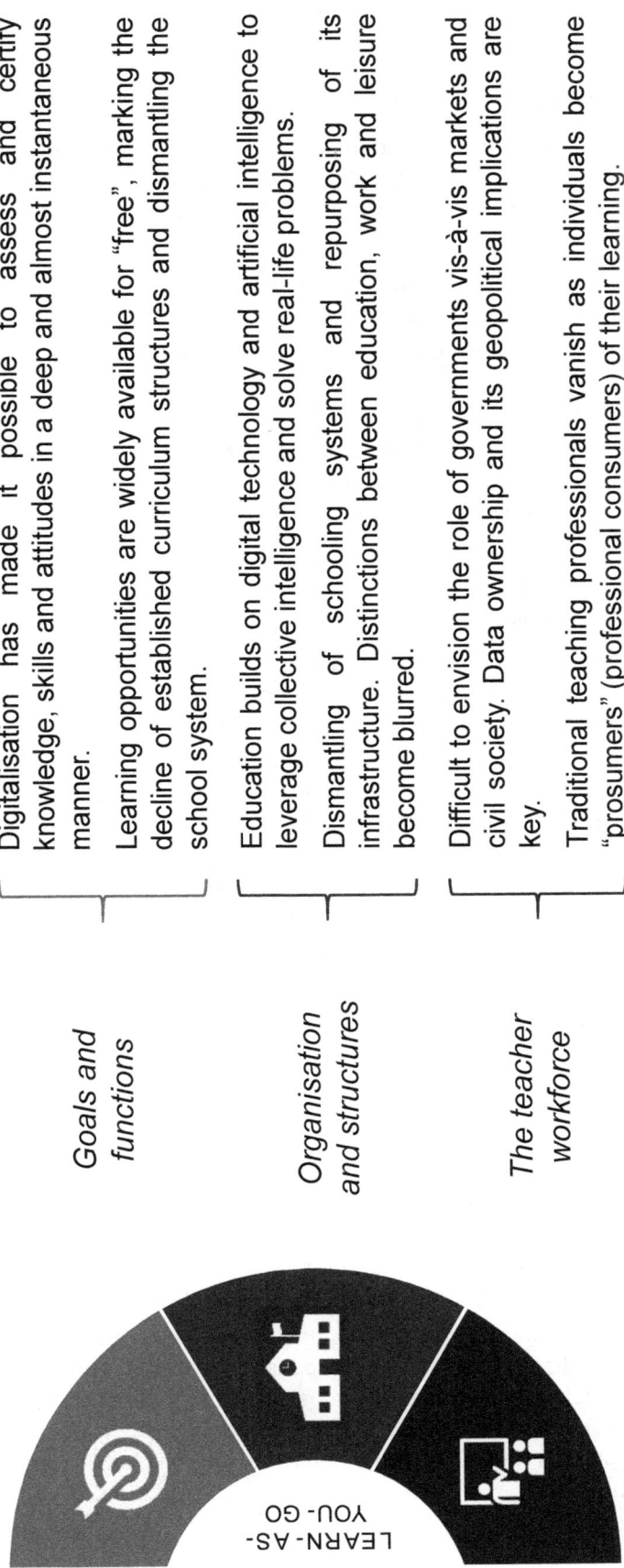

LEARN-AS-YOU-GO

Goals and functions

Digitalisation has made it possible to assess and certify knowledge, skills and attitudes in a deep and almost instantaneous manner.

Learning opportunities are widely available for "free", marking the decline of established curriculum structures and dismantling the school system.

Organisation and structures

Education builds on digital technology and artificial intelligence to leverage collective intelligence and solve real-life problems.

Dismantling of schooling systems and repurposing of its infrastructure. Distinctions between education, work and leisure become blurred.

The teacher workforce

Difficult to envision the role of governments vis-à-vis markets and civil society. Data ownership and its geopolitical implications are key.

Traditional teaching professionals vanish as individuals become "prosumers" (professional consumers) of their learning.

Governance and geopolitics

- Deinstitutionalisation of public education, dismantling of schooling.
- (Global) governance of data and digital technologies potentially key.

Challenges for public authorities

- High risk of social fragmentation.
- Potentially high interventionism (state, corporate) in all areas of life.
- Tensions around democratic control and protection of individual rights.

Box 4.5. Using the scenarios: Learn-as-you-go

Signals from the present and questions for discussion

We are currently experiencing enormous interest and investment in digitalisation and artificial intelligence. With the rise of machine learning, there is also growing curiosity to learn from the high tech sector itself (Williamson, 2016[7]). Combined, these are strong signals from the present that Scenario 4 could come to fruition.

- With the rise of artificial intelligence, big data and sophisticated search algorithms, do learners need to learn facts anymore? What consequences would there be if they would not?

- Who is auditing the algorithms? Could we imagine a time when auditing algorithms is considered a basic civic duty, like serving as a juror for a trial, for example? Or could it already be built in to the development process, i.e. "justice by design"?

- Provided that massive student data collection could safeguard individual privacy, could student data become a new source of revenue for schooling systems, leveraging the interest of high tech venture capital in feeding the learning of their "smart" machines?

Some examples of learning and skilling outside formal education and schooling are visible today, such as coding boot camps; or children who are "unschooled" – this is, a step beyond home education in the sense that children decide what they'd like to learn and when.

- What are some of the pros and cons of having a common curriculum? Does the absence of formal curricula expand learners' freedom and autonomy? What about common values and social habits, common areas of knowing and understanding?

- The absence of powerful external motivators – such as mandatory schooling, school disciplinary regimes and teacher praise – may require this future to develop alternative forms of motivating learners. Could this be embedding learning by design in entertainment platforms? Linking skilling programmes to social entitlements? Something else?

- Teachers regularly express their preference for collaborative forms of professional development that build on their daily practice. Could "teacher boot camps" (where learning builds mainly on hands-on work and interactions among participants) be the future of professional development? Would these be very different from professional conventions in other professions?

A last signal from the present is increasingly embedding technologies in our lives (and our bodies). Digital personal assistants, smart toys and wearable devices have all changed the way we interact with learning and technology in our daily lives.

- If a machine is responsible for our learning, does this scenario imply a powerful version of a "hidden curriculum"? A colonisation (by the state, corporations, or other groups) of socialisation processes currently transmitted by schools but also family, community and peers, the media?

- What would more personalised learning through technology entail for student experiences? Are learning personalisation and individualisation synonyms? How do the results of technology-led personalisation compare to more traditional forms of teacher-led personalisation?

- To what extent are the "personalised" learning technologies available today truly adaptive to individual students rather than more or less responsive forms of content management? Although in theory digital technologies make an almost infinite number of choices possible (e.g. in music, films, books, etc.), in practice the algorithms behind "you might also like" steer people to a particular subset of options. Could the same happen to learning content and pedagogies?

References

Loewus, L. (2017), *Schools Take a Page From Silicon Valley With 'Scrum' Approach - Education Week*, Education Week, https://www.edweek.org/ew/articles/2017/11/01/schools-take-a-page-from-silicon-valley.html (accessed on 6 May 2020).
[5]

Milord, J. (2019), *No degree? No problem. Here are the jobs at Top Companies you can land without one | LinkedIn*, LinkedIn, https://www.linkedin.com/pulse/degree-problem-you-can-still-land-jobs-top-companies-joseph-milord/ (accessed on 4 May 2020).
[4]

OECD (2019), *Trends Shaping Education 2019*, OECD Publishing, Paris, https://dx.doi.org/10.1787/trends_edu-2019-en.
[2]

OECD (2018), *Going digital in a multilateral world*, OECD, Paris, https://www.oecd.org/going-digital/C-MIN-2018-6-EN.pdf (accessed on 3 May 2020).
[6]

OECD (2001), *What Schools for the Future?*, Schooling for Tomorrow, OECD Publishing, Paris, https://dx.doi.org/10.1787/9789264195004-en.
[1]

Skidelsky, L. (2019), *How to achieve shorter working hours*, Progressive Economy Forum, London, https://progressiveeconomyforum.com/wp-content/uploads/2019/08/PEF_Skidelsky_How_to_achieve_shorter_working_hours.pdf (accessed on 27 May 2020).
[3]

Williamson, B. (2016), "Silicon startup schools: technocracy, algorithmic imaginaries and venture philanthropy in corporate education reform", *Critical Studies in Education*, Vol. 59/2, pp. 218-236, http://dx.doi.org/10.1080/17508487.2016.1186710.
[7]

5 Back from the future(s): Outcomes, implications and paradoxes

Imagining a future where massive schooling systems have radically transformed or, instead, have completely disappeared can be difficult. Our schools are deeply rooted in our societies and in our current ways of living, seeing and thinking. This closing chapter explores key elements and potential outcomes and implications of the four OECD Scenarios for the Futures of Schooling. It identifies seven tensions and paradoxes that must be considered when using the scenarios. Its aim is to highlight key challenges where further discussion can be most valuable.

Introduction

In all OECD countries, school systems currently employ large numbers of people, deploy vast sums of money, and oversee the education and care of millions of students. Despite the diversity of economic, technological and societal changes in the past decades, "the place called school" is still the dominant model for educating our youth, even if schools and schooling systems look different across the OECD.

Given the omnipresence of this model, imagining a future where massive schooling systems have radically transformed or, instead, have completely disappeared can be difficult. Our schools are deeply rooted in our societies and in our current ways of living, seeing and thinking. This can make using the scenarios an exercise of radical thinking and imagination. At the same time, both historical alternative forms of organising education and the increasingly complex and unpredictable world we live in today encourage us to make the effort. Indeed, we must not only reflect on the future of the system as we know it, we must also challenge ourselves to think of redistributing learning along the lifelong and life-wide dimensions.

Scenarios can help clarify main directions and offer strategic options for schooling over the long-term by exploring the policy issues that arise in different futures. This closing chapter explores the key dimensions and implications of the scenarios, and highlights tensions and paradoxes that must be considered when thinking about the future of schooling. It aims to push the reader to engage precisely with the elements that are most challenging, and where further discussion can be most valuable.

Continuity and disruption: Dimensions and implications of the scenarios

Schooling became the vast institutional system we know today because of its capacity to deliver on a number of important societal goals and functions, from teaching and learning to children's care. There is no better evidence of schooling's success than to see how fundamental schools are in the daily life of our communities. Imagining a future in which the goals and functions that schools serve are met differently can thus only be a demanding exercise.

Nevertheless, the scenarios in this report demonstrate that developments within education itself, government and the wider society may result in other – more or less plausible – structures to address social needs. In the end, the value of schooling and schools is dependent on ongoing subjective evaluations (moral, political, instrumental, aesthetical) and, as such, may evolve along with broader contextual changes (Meynhardt, 2009[1]).

Exploring the dimensions that currently characterise schooling allows for a systematic consideration of how they could be altered and combined in alternative futures. This section explores these dimensions for schooling's organisation and structures, human resources and governance processes.

What future for schools and schooling?

As noted by Selwyn (2011[2]), school and schooling encompass different things. *School* is the institution where learners do their learning and teachers do their teaching, whereas *schooling* refers to the processes of learning or teaching at school. The idea of the school as an institution includes both its physical and cultural structures defined by a series of roles and rules, such as "the hierarchical roles that people assume within the school organisation, the hierarchies of knowledge that constitutes the school curriculum, and the organisation of time that constitutes the school timetable" (Selwyn, 2011, p. 141[2]). The process of schooling, on the other hand, can be understood as including explicit processes such as different combinations of teaching and learning, communication and decision-making as well as implicit processes of socialisation, regulation and control. The scenarios can be analysed against four ideal types emerging from a four-quadrant matrix, where schools and schooling are both defined in terms of continuity or transformation (Figure 5.1).

Figure 5.1. What futures for schools and schooling?

Continuity and discontinuity of education structures (schools) and processes (schooling)

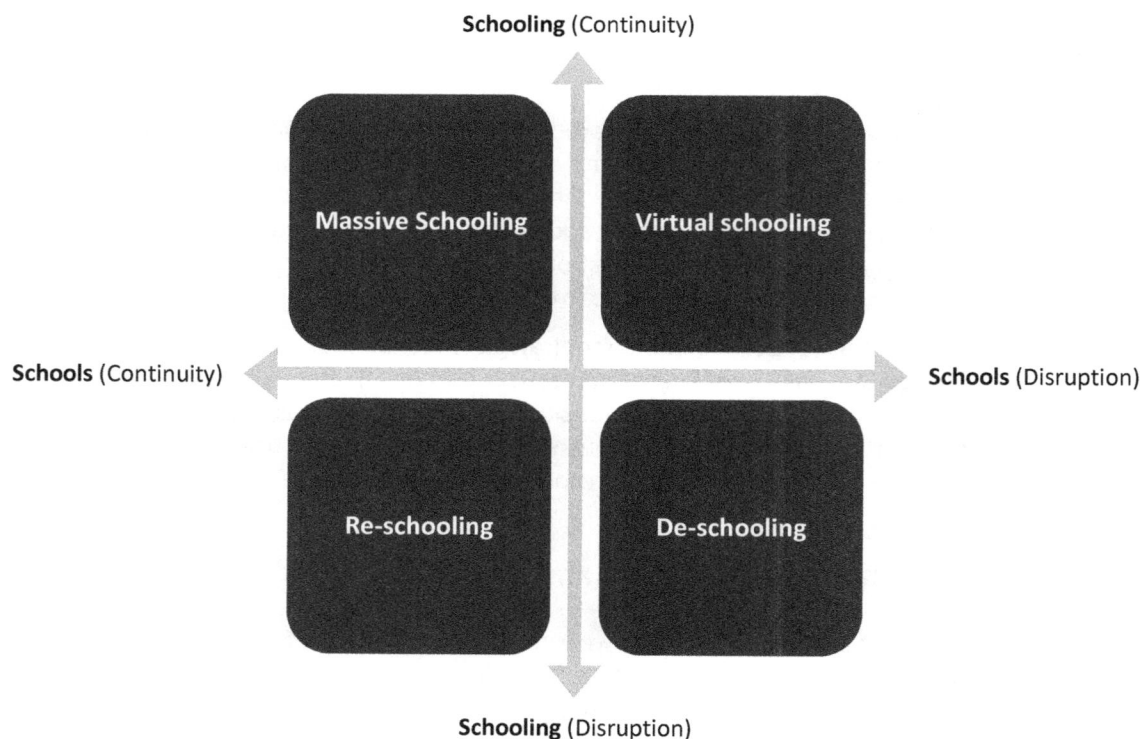

Source: Selwyn (2011[2])

- *Massive schooling*: implies the continuity of both schools and schooling as we know them. Its version of the future is characterised by continuing increase in participation in formal education. Although modernised by technology, learners and teachers continue to operate within rather uniform structures and standardised processes. Open questions are whether and how this could extend beyond traditional schooling (e.g. to early childhood education and care, lifelong learning).

- *Virtual schooling*: Here "virtual" is not restricted to digital learning only. Schooling continues, but learners do their learning and teachers do their teaching outside the confines of conventional physical schools, within a context of flexible relationships and greater choice (of sources for learning, of learning objectives, etc.). But the transformation of the physical space does not automatically imply very different processes of teaching and learning if the choice is to mix and blend components and modules that are mainly standardised (Leadbeater, 2006[3]). It does not automatically follow that innovation would be common either. As noted by Bentley and Miller, an "ironic outcome of private sector firms' experiences with "mass customisation" has been the response of consumers to the immense range of choices they were offered. [...] in most cases consumers selected from within a narrow range" (2006, p. 118[4]).

- *Re-schooling*: Schools continue, but schooling changes. The attainment of shared core academic knowledge and skills may endure, but these are not necessarily pursued through common processes. Traditional roles and relationships in schools change, including those of and between teachers and students. This future could fluidly include multiple educational sectors, including vocational education and training (VET), early childhood education and care, formal tertiary and both formal and informal lifelong learning.

- *De-schooling:* The structures and processes of both schooling and schools are disrupted. This future has completely transformed teaching and learning as we know it and traditional notions of physical infrastructure, curriculum and qualifications are all overridden. Current distinctions between educational sectors (including VET, early childhood education and care, formal tertiary and both formal and informal lifelong learning) are no longer institutionalised.

Using the scenarios: Schools and schooling

Scenarios 1 and 2 of the OECD scenarios (see Chapter 4) extrapolate elements of the status quo, where formal education is delivered through a single organisation framework – schooling systems, virtual or not – and the continuation of traditional processes, such as a pre-eminence of curricula and national and international benchmarking through assessments and formal credentials. While school structures may remain in scenario 2, this proposes combinations of face-to-face and distance relations. In addition, it foresees changes in schooling conventions, such as reworking traditional schedules and the organisation of learning institutions away from hierarchical working organisations.

To an extent, scenario 3 also offers discontinuity of schools, distributing its activity across different virtual and physical spaces, locally and/or internationally. Alternatively, scenario 3 could also be consistent with an extended school housing multiple activities (like many college campuses today) other than those purely academic; this possibility is also present in scenario 1. Nevertheless, unlike scenario 1, the re-schooling of scenario 3 means that traditional categories, divisions and stratification methods and standardised ways of doing in schools have paved the way for increased experimentation. This results in a diversity of arrangements, including pedagogical methods, teacher-student and school-community relations, and highly flexible curricula and grouping strategies.

The idea of de-schooling is also visible in the scenarios. This could be the case in scenario 2, if those individuals leaving traditional schools do not participate in the supply of virtual schooling, as it happens today with those engaged in unschooling. De-schooling is of course most notable in scenario 4, which assumes that modern forms of connectivity and multiple services delivery are powerful enough for the entire school system to disappear.

What futures for teachers and teaching?

The scenarios have different implications for teachers and teaching, ranging from distinct corps in bureaucratic systems and private learning contractors to networked professionals in flexible organisations. Istance and Mackay (2014[5]) offer two useful dimensions with which to explore possible futures for teachers: a) the extent to which those tasked with teaching work within schools and b) the extent to which these practitioners are highly-trained teaching professionals or rather encompass a wider range of professional profiles, careers and expertise. Organised in a four-quadrant matrix (Figure 5.2), they generate four ideal types.

- *Teachers in educational monopolies*: Schools remain the main vehicle for organising teaching and learning and a distinct teacher corps dominates within them. Being able to teach requires the acquisition of teacher status. Trained teachers remain the large majority of the educational workforce within schools, although schools may open to the participation of other adults and professionals in their day-to-day activities.
- *Specialist professionals as hubs in schools*: Schools retain their functions but a wide range of adults and professionals are also involved, including family members, learning professionals other than teachers (such as consultants external to schools), as well as community experts in fields other

than teaching and learning. The nature of participation ranges from volunteering to formal contracts, whether occasional or stable and long-term.

- *A system of licenced flexible expertise*: Liberalisation of the places where teaching and learning take place but strong regulatory control and formal teacher certification is required for teaching. However, different routes to acquiring teacher status may exist, either through significant or low investment in professional education and development. Professional licencing and control become main accountability measures, via direct intervention of the public administration or through strong professional bodies, which may also channel intense teacher networking – in this case outside schools – to avoid professional isolation.

- *In the open market*: This assumes a de-schooling future, where schools and teachers have lost their monopolies. Multiple learning suppliers and contractors are in charge of teaching. They could operate via a form of laissez-faire, with no requirement for formal certification, or also develop within a context where, while teaching and learning methods and means are flexible, a number of tests and credentials still act as quality controls and currency in the learning market.

Figure 5.2. What futures for teachers and teaching?

Mapping the future of teaching across location and the agent of teaching

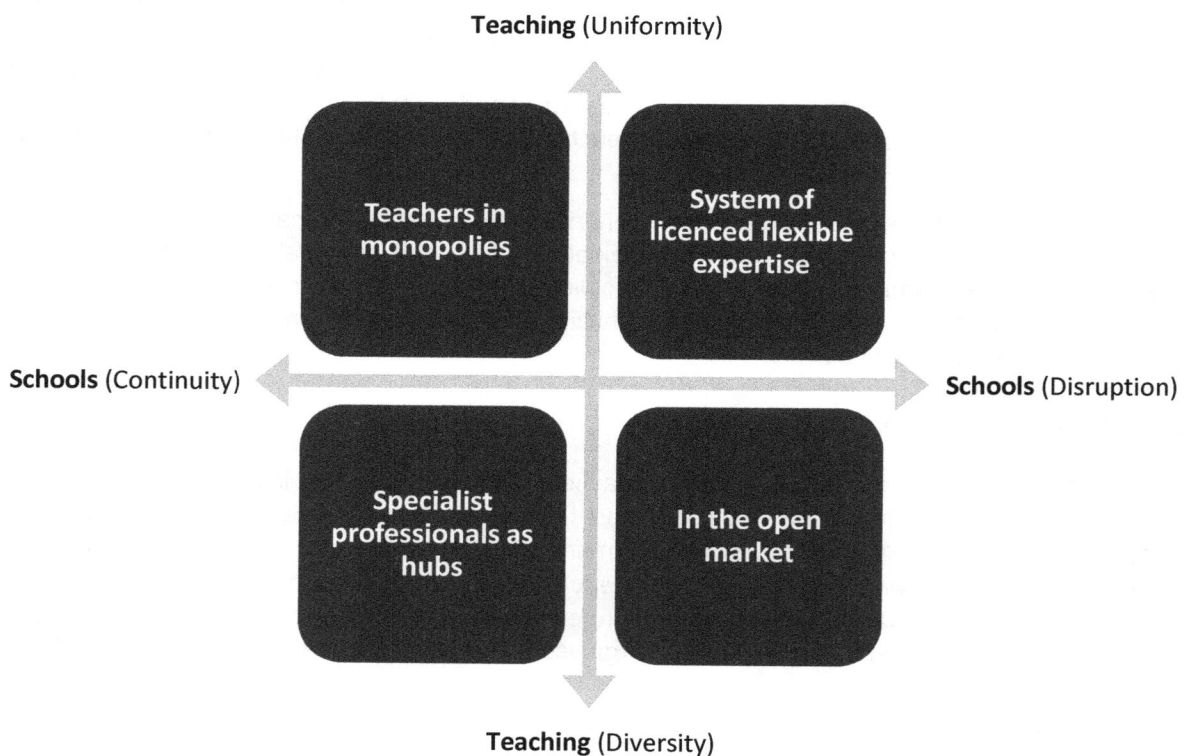

Source: Istance and Mackay (2014[5])

Using the scenarios: Teachers and teaching

The four OECD scenarios do not align directly with the ideal types presented above. This is reasonable to the extent that these options are already present in the educational landscape today. Distinct teacher corps remain the main source of teaching in schools but new sources of learning are also increasingly present, with formal academic institutions no longer acting as gatekeepers of knowledge due to an explosion in learning sources across multiple actors and places. Scenario 1 reflects this idea under the assumption of closer links with digital learning providers operating outside schools. Scenario 3 goes one step further in assuming a much wider and flexible diversification of the sources for teaching, situating itself closely to the idea of a teaching that operates through professionals as hubs. In this sense, scenario 3 is an extrapolation of those schools that already make systematic use of learning resources and experts in their environment, from bringing professionals of various fields into the school to talk to students to partnering with using public spaces other than schools (e.g. museums) to conduct lessons.

Scenario 2 remains open on this dimension. A diversity of professionals could operate in (digital) learning platforms, but also these would benefit from trained teachers to do the teaching and participate in the design of the platform itself. Scenario 2, like scenario 4, opens the door to teaching that is not governed by professional arrangements. Occurring "in the open market", it could involve forms of private tutoring and informal lecturing already present today. In scenario 2, however, quality assurance mechanisms such as assessments require the agreement of educational professionals for their design and marking.

An additional element to consider is the impact of digital technology on teaching. Reflecting on education and technology, Selwyn (2011[2]) provides a synthesis of the main views on this issue:

- A first view considers technology's potential to enhance teaching and pedagogy. The increasing ability of technology to automate bureaucratic and administrative workload, increased access to a plethora of instructional tools and ways of delivery, and the new channels and sources to (collaborative) professional development could free-up time for teachers to focus on students' needs while providing powerful tools and the knowledge to do so.

- A second view sees increasingly digitalised and automated education processes leading to the disappearance of the traditional teacher. While not foreseeing the complete replacement of teachers and other forms of tutoring, this implies a substantial reduction in the human resources required to deliver education programmes.

- In between these two perspectives, a third view sees a future where the role of teachers changes. Here, technology facilitates more learner-directed learning, which implies that teaching shifts from directing learning experiences to designing and facilitating them.

These three views are reflected in the scenarios, although they could play out in different ways. Technology could liberate teachers from some non-teaching tasks in scenario 1, although it could also become a source of de-professionalisation, particularly in scenario 1 if teachers are relegated to contingency management in classrooms. Scenario 3 openly assumes the in-between option of shifting roles, roles that could be played similarly by public learning councillors and private contractors in scenario 2. Scenario 4 goes a step further to paint a future where formal teaching is no longer in demand.

What role for education authorities?

The governance of education is another important dimension, with diverse actors operating on multiple layers of influence and decision-making: local, regional, national and supranational; private and public, with greater voice for parents and other actors in civil society. An analytical framework for exploring the evolution of education governance (Frankowski et al., 2018[6]), yields the four approaches presented as a matrix in Figure 5.3. All of the approaches currently exist in some version in OECD countries, although the last 30 years have seen a move from public administration to new public management, which in turn evolved into network governance in many systems.

- The traditional public administration perspective centres the role of government on legality and the rule of law. Public goals are determined in political processes, and policies are formulated for translating political decision into concrete actions. Civil servants execute and perform these policies, ensuring the standardisation of response by government.

- The *new public management* (NPM) perspective is oriented towards efficient and effective policy execution, incorporating corporate-like management ideas into the governance of public services. This view is characterised by tools such as performance targets, deregulation, efficiency, contract management, and financial control.

- A *network governance* view focuses on networks and partnerships. Emerging from increasing decentralisation and the consequently reduced role of central educational authorities, it assumes the participation of multiple stakeholders in decision-making and policy implementation and a civil service that is required to actively work towards building alliances, transcending its "silos".

- The *societal resilience* perspective sees public value emerging within the bounds of government responsibility, but societal actors are the ones primarily responsible for its definition and production, guided by their own preferences and priorities. It works through self-organised networks and cooperatives.

Figure 5.3. What future for education governance?

Governance across roles (government vs society) and the nature of effort (value vs. results)

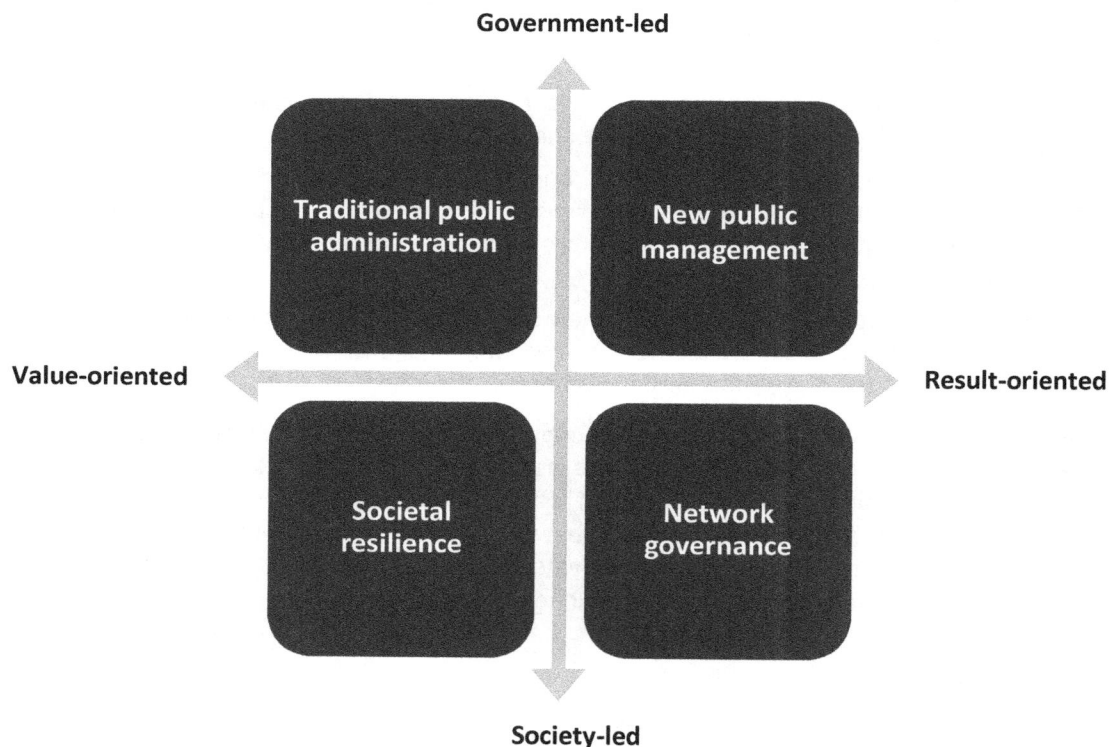

Source: Frankowski et al. (2018[6])

Using the scenarios: Education governance and the role of public authorities

The OECD scenarios presented in the previous chapter acknowledge that all four governance approaches may continue to be visible and intertwined in the organisation of schooling. Rather, standardised governance approaches, such as massive schooling in scenario 1, can be an effective means to ensure access and quality of education provision for all. A more dynamic education provision landscape, such as that of scenario 2, in fact makes regulatory roles essential to safeguard the right to education. A legalistic view could also be key to ensuring child rights and inclusiveness in systems where a strong central bureaucracy had lost its influence, such as in scenario 3, or to increase transparency and public value behind the "algorithmocracy" suggested in scenario 4.

Critics of the new public management agenda have highlighted its failure to deliver massive-scale innovation through market-based models and the larger inequities and costs that have come with expanded parental school choice and demand-oriented school planning. However, such criticisms do not imply that the future will inevitably act as a pendulum, bringing systems back to a radical centralised/communitarian perspective (Theisens, 2016[7]). Parental choice, for example, is in many instances considered an intrinsic value rather than simply a means to an end; perhaps increasingly so as highly educated parents become more involved in their children's education, as seen in scenario 2. Growing public and private investment in learning metrics suggests a future in which measuring results plays a larger, not a smaller role.

From providing new digital tools and educational resources internationally in a massive schooling model, for example in scenario 1, to optimising educational infrastructure and professional knowledge in strong local ecosystems, for example in scenario 3, networks and partnerships between multiple actors can continue to be expected as means for education actors to mobilise knowledge and expertise to define and solve their common challenges. This, as suggested by the societal resilience approach, may increasingly occur through the direct involvement and self-organisation of citizens themselves, although alliances with other actors, such as corporate digital services and others, like healthcare providers, may grow increasingly common, as suggested by the network governance perspective.

The future of schooling: goals, tensions and paradoxes

The goals and functions of education are complex and intertwined

The goals of education are intertwined with the daily reality of schools and take different shapes and weights depending on each specific context. Child care and safety are the first priority for many parents who need to balance working and family life, especially for younger children. For others, reduced school hours can work well as long as more flexible working arrangements or sufficient social and financial capital permit them to fulfil this role outside the framework of schooling. These multiple equilibria are in constant mutation as the nature of families itself evolves: with the nuclear family (married heterosexual couple with children) becoming less common; the number of reconstituted and single-parent households rising; overall families becoming smaller and individuals deciding to have children later in life, if at all (OECD, 2016[8]).

Education is also the means for individuals to acquire professional and personal competencies and to develop as independent citizens. This entails building the cognitive, social and emotional skills needed for a world of rapid change where students enter increasingly diverse careers. This is an enormous challenge, as schools face growing demands to provide all students with greater technical skills and an ever-growing base of academic knowledge at the same time as they are expected to help students develop careful reflection, critical analysis and diverse, creative forms of expressivity.

To complicate things further, knowledge and skills acquired through schooling risk becoming quickly outdated in an age where knowledge grows exponentially and labour market expectations are diverse and rapidly shifting. Traditionally, formal assessment, qualifications and career and academic guidance systems have played a key function validating what learners know and can do. These have allowed society to effectively allocate skills in the economy. Increasingly, however, education systems need to move from a front-loaded model – in which individuals develop and acquire skills and knowledge exclusively in their earlier years – to one based on lifelong learning, which allows individuals to pursue diverse learning trajectories throughout their academic and professional lives.

While there is a greater volume and range of participation in adult learning than there used to be, in most countries the goal of lifelong learning is still distant. In addition, despite a recognition that schools are essential to this goal (Faure et al., 1972[9]), at least in the 15-20 year future on which this report focuses, there has yet to be a fundamental re-think of what the distinct role of schools would need to be to meet this challenge.

What we understand as schooling today will continue to exist in the future as long as individuals find it valuable (for academic learning and personal and civic development, care, socialisation and certification). In an increasingly networked and diverse society, the future of institutionalised education will depend on its ability to bridge different worlds, and to remain relevant to the needs of individuals and society.

Seven tensions and paradoxes

Modernising vs. Disrupting

There is a fundamental question about whether our vision for the future of schooling is understood as an incremental process of modernising and/or whether it involves radical disruptive transformation. Consider for example how teaching and learning could evolve in schools and classrooms fully equipped with cutting-edge technology, able to capture body information, facial expressions or neural signals. Would the extremely precise insights on student emotional states generated by these tools be used to transform teaching, reorganise learning, collaborative work and relationships among actors (students, teachers, parents)? Or would it rather be used to incrementally modernise existing practices, feeding in to traditional assessment mechanisms, or even potentially moulding students towards pre-established "norms" of behaviour, for example stereotyped ways of behaving (Knox, Williamson and Bayne, 2019[10])? Although technology is often considered as synonymous with innovation and transformational change, examples of it being used to disrupt, rather than adapt and modernise, are not common in education.

Another, more challenging, example of the modernising vs. disrupting tension is that of lifelong learning. There is a long-standing recognition of the need to integrate school policy and practice into the larger lifelong learning framework, especially as our societies continue to age (Istance, 2015[11]). Despite this, formal education continues to offer more training early in life and career, when an individual is less experienced, while offering less later, when they have more experience. The quality and suitability of this offer is also questioned. The current approach of making incremental changes to existing structures has not yet solved the problem, and in many ways it cannot be expected to, given the difficulty in effectively shifting well-entrenched systems.

So what would it take to really make lifelong learning fit for purpose? Fundamentally different learning approaches? Breaking down barriers between work and "learning" to create a seamless series of opportunities to develop as a professional? Specific assigned periods throughout the lifespan where individuals develop their personal and professional skill set, unrelated to their employment or employer? More equal distribution of and access to quality resources and opportunities early on in life? Changing minds and habits so that individuals have a "thirst for learning" across the lifespan and along the entire continuum between work and leisure (Sivan and Stebbins, 2011[12]; OECD, 2019[13])? The scenarios suggest contrasting possibilities such as shorter, more intensive school careers on one hand and an extended initial education on the other; or greater flexibility in learning paths as opposed to highly focused academic careers.

Cutting-edge technology and lifelong learning are just two examples of the most fundamental tension underlying our thinking about the future of education. Note that there is not one right answer: in some circumstances modernising is called for, while in others real disruption is required. What is important to keep in mind is that modernising can and does masquerade as disruption. If disruption is called for, it will require completely different ways of thinking and engagement to deliver. This is extremely difficult to do well, and requires not just political arguments to free resources and set the stage for potentially radical structural changes/policies to implement, but also challenging world views and creating new ways of thinking.

New goals vs. Old structures

As the goals and purposes of education evolve, they can become disconnected from the processes and structures under which it operates. One clear example of this is that while there is widespread agreement on the need to personalise learning experiences to individual needs, many also agree that among the skills and attitudes most needed are co-operation and team-work (Deming, 2017[14]; Weidmann, Deming and School, 2020[15]). Indeed, very few students across the OECD can handle problem-solving tasks that require them to maintain awareness of group dynamics, take the initiative to overcome obstacles, and resolve disagreements and conflicts (OECD, 2017[16]). Importantly, the relationship between collaborative capacities and strong academic performance is not direct: while the absence of basic academic skills does not imply the presence of social and emotional skills, social skills are not an automatic result of the development of academic skills either.

Aligning the goals and means in education is necessary if different objectives are to be met. At the same time, we must also acknowledge that more fundamental tensions exist, possibly harder to circumvent. For instance, schooling is often described by its egalitarian aims, including those of access to learning for all and the development of a democratic citizenry. Similarly, education is key to social mobility – despite existing gaps in education and skills across social groups, students from disadvantaged backgrounds benefit more from participation in formal education than their advantaged peers.

Despite their equalising aims, schools are sorting machines, assessing and grouping individuals into formal and informal categories, such as enrolment processes, academic tracks, age grades, classrooms and ability groups and different academic paths. The social categories they construct provide a context for the formation of student identity, but also constitute drivers of inequality insofar as these shape the resources, incentives and expectations for and of students (Domina, Penner and Penner, 2017[17]).

Furthermore, while schooling is seen as an equaliser, its single organisational framework cannot be neutral to those it serves. The expectations around knowledge and skills (curriculum) and about social rules and roles that schools assume cannot be experienced the same way by all learners. Some learners find such expectations aligned with those of home and the community, while others experience them as completely separate worlds. These differences determine the way learners approach and go through their life at school, including academic performance, engagement and sense of belonging at school (OECD, 2018[18]).

A question for the future of schooling and education more broadly thus relates to whether massive schooling systems will be capable of disrupting the inequalities that they contribute to create in the first place, including the decoupling of their dividing lines from later-life outcomes, and whether potential alternatives to schooling would succeed in their stead. Another question is how education is conceived in the wider social, economic and cultural environment, and whether massive schooling or other forms of education are able to make up for the social inequalities that extend well beyond the education system – and that education can only compensate for to a certain extent.

Global vs. Local

The future of schooling will depend on the degree of consensus or conflict over goals, the level of (dis)satisfaction, recognition and esteem in which they are held. Much has been made of the open and participatory governance mechanisms that aim to improve shared vision and ownership by involving a wide variety of stakeholders in the policy-making process. However, because public value creation is dependent on diverging and sometimes conflicting perspectives, tensions and inconsistencies arise around national (or even international) priorities versus local ones. This plays out in multiple ways. One example is accountability, and the processes defining, measuring and evaluating schools' goals and schools' capacity to meet them. As demands on schools grow, and with them the cost of failure, how can the need for accountability to system-wide goals be assured without its mechanisms undermining the local flexibility and resulting quality of education that they are intended to promote (Burns, Köster and Fuster, 2016[19])?

In addition, although schools in many countries are often evaluated mainly by their academic output, a key function of education is socialisation and the development of citizens. Many systems are implementing accountability systems that hold schools accountable for multiple outcomes beyond the academic, with local actors setting their own priorities and identifying their own needs. However, these must coexist with national goals and expectations, and there is an inherent tension between responsive local flexibility and ensuring national standards for all. Who determines what is measured, and whose voice counts (most)?

Accountability is an integral feature of all the scenarios, although the mechanisms through which it is realised differ across them: from an approach based on the close monitoring of performance and attainment, to the accountability generated in the exercise of user choice, to that exerted by local participation in decision-making as means of quality control. Even scenario 4, where a process of de-institutionalisation has taken place, raises questions about power distribution and accountability with notable ethical and political implications, such as those for privacy and transparency, for data ownership and school funding (Williamson, 2015[20]; 2016[21]).

Another example of the tension between national (or even international) priorities versus local ones is curriculum content, for example in languages. Many systems prioritise the need to learn skills for a changing labour market, strengthening instruction of English and other powerful languages of business and global markets. Yet at the same time, there are concerns about preserving local heritage and worries about languages and cultures disappearing as rural youth migrate to larger cities where they no longer use the language of their ancestors. What is the best way to balance these divergent needs? How will the global reach of the Internet impact on this tension (on the one hand, powerful global languages like English are becoming even more widespread as content is shared digitally; on the other, the Internet also allows for greater sharing of local content, including documenting the remaining speakers of disappearing languages and perhaps protecting their legacy)? This tension is present in all of the four scenarios, whether it plays out on regional and national levels or supranationally.

Innovation vs. Risk avoidance

Improving the functioning of public services requires innovation, and the ability to change and evolve with new circumstances and challenges. Innovation in turn requires risk-taking – trying something new, and possibly, failing. In education, there is a push to make our systems more innovative and our teachers more creative. Yet making this happen is no easy task. Countries must encourage innovation in their education systems at the same time as their accountability systems seek to minimise risk and error. This is an important and difficult tension: Reconciling risk and innovation constitutes a demanding challenge (Burns and Blanchenay, 2016[22]; Brown and Osborne, 2013[23]).

Education systems remain too often stuck in a paradigm of risk minimisation. While understandable, not only does this restrict innovation and change, it also ignores a fundamental truth: that the status quo can be risky to maintain. No change is also a decision that carries consequences. What is the cost of inaction, or of not improving methods/strategies/approaches? Most often, this cost is simply not known, or not calculated. While this might be politically expedient (and the safest path), it transfers the risk and the costs of inaction or failure to those the system is supposed to serve, i.e. the learners.

However, education systems must accept that taking risks means that there is a possibility of failure. This cannot be avoided, and in fact it would be unwise to minimise this possibility, both in the public discussion surrounding policy choices and in the reaction to a failed initiative. Failure can and should be used as a learning tool, both for scientific purposes (understanding what works and what does not) and for political ones (resources can be wasted if the appropriate lessons are not drawn from failures) (Burns and Blanchenay, 2016[22]; Blanchenay and Burns, 2016[24]).

In the scenarios, the continuation of massive schooling of scenario 1 may be seen as a sign of inaction and conservatism. On the other hand, the risks of fragmentation and superficial innovation that could result from the other scenarios should be no less of a concern. One further aspect to consider is the impact of the massive digitalisation of schooling and the resulting constant flow of data from which to assess what works and what does not. How useful would such data be, both in terms of their validity and whether or not they are able to be used, given current disputes and challenges?

Potential vs. Reality

All the scenarios in this volume propose an important role for technology in future articulations of school and schooling, although to various degrees and specificities. Strong tensions lie in this assumption, not least because using technology well for pedagogical purposes has consistently proven to be an elusive task. The key to breaking this pattern requires integrating technology into the complex contexts – and their constraints – where teachers and learners operate.

Technology has historically carried the hopes of many to transform education, by either refining teaching and learning in school or removing the need for schooling entirely. Back in 1920s and 30s, for instance, some saw radio and television as a way to mainstream educational programmes (Novak, 2012[25]). More recently, computers and the Internet have been touted as a solution to a host of educational weaknesses, in particular the ability to overcome long-standing criticisms of rigid and standardised instruction through varied and personalised learning.

However, to date evidence of the ability of technology to effectively transform teaching and learning has been scarce (Escueta et al., 2017[26]; Higgins, Xiao and Katsipataki, 2012[27]). Despite its potential, it has become clear that, irrespective of the sophistication of the technology applied, technology itself has not enhanced learning. One reason for this may be that EdTech programmes and platforms tend to reinforce rather than reframe existing pedagogical approaches. Another is that they are often designed based on developer and market ideas, unconnected to educational and pedagogical goals and learning science research. An additional challenge emerges when technology is promoted for classrooms without appropriate pedagogical consideration (OECD, 2018[28]). A limited use of technology by teachers is not necessarily due to conservatism, but may reflect teachers' expert judgement of the opportunity costs that technology integration entails – in terms of time spent and the perceived effects on learning outcomes.

The emergence of Artificial Intelligence (AI) has renewed the hopes for the transformational promise of educational technology. Today, digital learning systems powered by increasingly 'smart' algorithms and education data mining have the potential to provide all learners with access to almost unlimited instructional strategies while guiding and supporting their learning along the way (Luckin et al., 2016[29]; Luckin, 2018[30]).

However, leaving potential aside, a clear tension lies in the discourse around learning "personalisation", and whether emerging technologies could potentially bring learners to the standardised place from which "edTech" was supposed to liberate them in the first place. Existing "personalised" learning technologies can range from simple customisation of a learning interface to systems that adapt content delivery depending upon user performance (Bulger, 2016[31]). While the latter is not in itself negative, if increased insights on learners' experience are used solely as means to optimise factory-like processes of incremental knowledge acquisition or to diminish teachers' role and thus the quality of education provision (The Institute for Ethical AI in Education, n.d.[32]), there is nothing transformative about it. More clarity is needed on what personalisation means and the extent to which existing forms of technology-enabled learning actually deliver it – and whether they add value to existing forms of teacher-delivered learning personalisation.

Virtual vs. Face-to-face

Just as scenarios push us to think further about the spaces and times for learning, they also help us examine the different physical modalities of teaching and learning. The more learning opportunities become accessible outside "the walls" of school, the more we must reflect on the role of face-to-face interaction and physical presence.

On the level of instruction, teacher effectiveness; instructor training and conformability with the technology used, support provided to students are key elements regardless of the method of delivery. Effective distance learning systems have the capacity to create the conditions for student-centred content, student-instructor and peer-to-peer interactions (Ellis-Thompson et al., 2020[33]; Abrami et al., 2011[34]).

Socially, however, studies comparing digital and face-to-face communication consistently find that in-person communication is more impactful in strengthening and maintaining relationships (Finkenauer et al., 2019[35]). In schools, this is visible in the warm and supportive relationships between teachers and learners as well as in student peer relations and co-operation, all of which are key to teaching, learning and well-being (OECD, 2019[36]). Yet, the counterfactual is also true: digital connection can also empower disadvantaged groups by enhancing weak ties, and connecting marginalised or minority youth with support that they might not have in their immediate physical community. Similarly, not all forms of physicality are necessarily pleasant: students may well be disengaged during lessons and peer interactions can be harmful, for example in bullying.

The distinction between on and offline will continue to become increasingly blurred. Digital technologies tend to supplement existing face-to-face friendships rather than replacing them, with online communication reinforcing offline friendships (Mesch, 2019[37]). When moving towards more flexible forms of schooling, such as those proposed in digital and blended learning, the tensions related to physicality and distance, autonomy and support, need to be carefully considered (OECD, 2018[38]).

Opening up schooling systems, such as by placing schools in larger learning ecosystems (scenario 3), could be an avenue to optimise resources and provide learners with more situated and deeper learning experiences. Key to consider, however, is the traditional role of physical schools as places where students encounter others very different from themselves. This allows them to experience not just difference, but also learn social scripts, either explicitly or implicitly. Cultivating familiarly and comfort with difference, and the tolerance that emerges with this, is an important role of schools and schooling. How this would be accomplished in virtual spaces where algorithms tend to sort us into groups with similar likes and attitudes is a difficult question.

Learning vs. Education

It has long been recognised that learning does not happen only in schools and other formal educational institutions. Learning also takes place both formally and informally in the context of the family and other social relations; through play, sport and volunteering; in the hands-on tasks of work and even the most casual of conversations. The more knowledge is accessible through multiple forms and channels – such as nowadays being available at the touch of a screen – the less realistic it is to conceive of educational institutions as its sole gatekeeper.

However, ours is a time that has been characterised as one of 'enlightened illiteracy' (Garcés, 2017[39]), where we can know everything about the world and yet do little about it. A key paradox is that the more we "know", the easier it becomes for us to succumb to our biases, using new knowledge just to validate those ideas of the world that we already have. Another paradox is that the more accessible knowledge becomes the more difficult it is to generate our own understanding of the world, resulting in an uncritical adherence to the opinions already available elsewhere.

Of utmost importance to a digitalised information society is to see that what distinguishes opinions from knowledge is not truth or utility. An opinion, a piece of information may be true and useful for decision-making regardless of whether its possessor has an understanding of its logic and applicability. Knowledge requires instead reasons or evidence to be sustained. Acquiring knowledge requires the skills for exploring, discerning and successfully employing good reasons to sustain a claim; elements that benefit from expert guidance and social interaction in addition to information access.

Beyond improving learners' knowledge of facts and figures in various disciplines, and adaptive learning tools can have a role to play in this, teaching works towards enhancing learners' understanding of knowledge and the ways to develop it (Hofer and Pintrich, 2002[40]) and mobilising the motivational resources necessary for this process to happen. As discussed, disconnecting education's purposes and means can be problematic. The strength of schooling, and certain pedagogies (Paniagua and Istance, 2018[41]; Pellegrino, 2017[42]), lies in its power to transform practices such as inquiry, reflection and cross-examination of ideas into habits, i.e. routine ways of doing, while continuing to promote a baseline of disciplinary and interdisciplinary knowledge on which to ground and develop such practices.

Once this role of teaching and pedagogy is recognised, teaching becomes even more critical to the success of schooling as expectations about quality increase: more demand-oriented approaches and less supply determined; more active and less passive learning; knowledge creation not just transmission. The profile, role, status, and rewards of teachers differ significantly between the scenarios, and some of the scenarios imply changes that may prove uncomfortable to teachers and to society. What impact would it have to massively involve adults other than teachers in the delivery of education, for example in scenario 3, and why has it not happened yet if considered beneficial? On the other hand, to what extent would closing the door to human tutoring (here potentially scenario 2 and 4, but also 1) open multiple windows to exclusion? The narrative of teacher disappearance risks becoming a self-fulfilling prophecy if policies and planning do not take into account all the functions of schooling and the value that teachers generate in them.

Coda

The different aspects of schooling and its goals do not always go together coherently or, in fact, support each other. Quite the contrary. Just as there is no "one" future, there is no single path that can or must be taken towards the futures of education. Each OECD country and community is responsible for defining the way ahead for their schools and their education systems more broadly. Nevertheless, as countries prepare for an increasingly uncertain future, a number of tensions and questions will need to be addressed. Some are long-standing issues, not yet sufficiently addressed, such as the function and place of massive schooling systems. Others are emerging and their impact is still uncertain, such as the role of artificial intelligence in delivering – or determining? – the future of education. This report, and the scenarios presented in Chapter 4, offer an opportunity for policymakers and stakeholders to reflect on these issues.

Underscoring many of the tensions presented in this report is the necessity for resources and investment in education – direct funding, professional expertise, technical infrastructure and facilities, parental and community engagement. Outcomes depend partly on their levels, but also on how such diverse resources are combined, used, and managed. To various degrees, all the scenarios are consistent with a diversification of the resource base. Relevant questions include: are societies willing to invest sufficiently in schools for the tasks expected of them? Can existing resources invested in schools be better integrated and optimised with those invested elsewhere? Could teachers and schools as well as education policy more widely address both formal and non-formal learning together to a greater extent?

Every government needs to prepare for the future. They have to consider not only the future changes that appear most probable, but also the changes that they are not already expecting, and the many ways in which the world could be very different to the one we live in today. They need to complement the evidence with a systematic consideration of future changes that cannot yet be captured in data—such as the unprecedented digital transformation of the global economy and society. They must transcend their own disciplines and silos, and discuss issues that may seem marginal but which in fact have significant potential implications. By systematically exploring different plausible futures and the opportunities and challenges they could present for education, we then use those ideas to make better decisions and act now.

In our rapidly changing world, education cannot rely on lessons of the past to prepare for the future. The future is here, and education systems need to learn from it. Our success will depend on how effectively we use our knowledge to anticipate the future, and how quickly we take action to shape it.

References

Abrami, P. et al. (2011), "Interaction in distance education and online learning: using evidence and theory to improve practice", *Journal of Computing in Higher Education*, Vol. 23/2-3, pp. 82-103, http://dx.doi.org/10.1007/s12528-011-9043-x. [34]

Bentley, T. and R. Miller (2006), "Personalisation: Getting the Questions Right", in *Personalising Education*, OECD Publishing, Paris, https://dx.doi.org/10.1787/9789264036604-9-en. [4]

Blanchenay, P. and T. Burns (2016), "Policy experimentation in complex education systems", in *Governing Education in a Complex World*, OECD Publishing, Paris, https://dx.doi.org/10.1787/9789264255364-10-en. [24]

Brown, L. and S. Osborne (2013), "Risk and Innovation", *Public Management Review*, Vol. 15/2, pp. 186-208, http://dx.doi.org/10.1080/14719037.2012.707681. [23]

Bulger, M. (2016), "Personalized learning: The conversations we're not having", *Data and Society*, Data and Society Research Institute, https://datasociety.net/wp-content/uploads/2016/09/PersonalizedLearning_primer_2016.pdf. [31]

Burns, T. and P. Blanchenay (2016), "Learning to fail, not failing to learn", in *Governing Education in a Complex World*, OECD Publishing, Paris, https://dx.doi.org/10.1787/9789264255364-12-en. [22]

Burns, T., F. Köster and M. Fuster (2016), *Education Governance in Action: Lessons from Case Studies*, Educational Research and Innovation, OECD Publishing, Paris, https://dx.doi.org/10.1787/9789264262829-en. [19]

Deming, D. (2017), "The growing importance of social skills in the labor market", *Quarterly Journal of Economics*, Vol. 132/4, pp. 1593-1640, http://dx.doi.org/10.1093/qje/qjx022. [14]

Domina, T., A. Penner and E. Penner (2017), "Categorical Inequality: Schools As Sorting Machines", *Annual Review of Sociology*, Vol. 43/1, pp. 311-330, http://dx.doi.org/10.1146/annurev-soc-060116-053354. [17]

Ellis-Thompson, A. et al. (2020), *Remote learning: Rapid evidence assessment*, Education Endowment Foundation, London, https://educationendowmentfoundation.org.uk/covid-19-resources/best-evidence-on-supporting-students-to-learn-remotely/ (accessed on 4 June 2020). [33]

Escueta, M. et al. (2017), "Education technology: An evidence-based review", *NBER Working Paper Series*, No. 23744, https://www.nber.org/papers/w23744.pdf. [26]

Faure, E. et al. (1972), *Learning to be: The world of education today and tomorrow*, International Commission on the Development of Education, UNESCO, https://unesdoc.unesco.org/ark:/48223/pf0000001801 (accessed on 14 November 2019). [9]

Finkenauer, C. et al. (2019), "The social context of adolescent relationships", in *Educating 21st Century Children: Emotional Well-being in the Digital Age*, OECD Publishing, Paris, https://dx.doi.org/10.1787/f71c8860-en. [35]

Frankowski, A. et al. (2018), "Dilemmas of central governance and distributed autonomy in education", *OECD Education Working Papers*, No. 189, OECD Publishing, Paris, https://dx.doi.org/10.1787/060260bf-en. [6]

Garcés, M. (2017), *New Radical Enlightenment [Nueva Ilustración Radical]*, Anagrama, Barcelona. [39]

Higgins, S., Z. Xiao and M. Katsipataki (2012), *The impact of digital technology on learning: A summary for the education endowment foundation*, Education Endowment Foundation and Durham University, Durham, https://educationendowmentfoundation.org.uk/evidence-summaries/evidence-reviews/digital-technology/. [27]

Hofer, B. and P. Pintrich (eds.) (2002), *Personal Epistemology: The Psychology of Beliefs about Knowledge and Knowing*, Routledge, New York and London. [40]

Istance, D. (2015), "Learning in retirement and old age: An agenda for the 21st century", *European Journal of Education*, Vol. 50/2, pp. 225-238, http://dx.doi.org/10.1111/ejed.12120. [11]

Istance, D. and A. Mackay (2014), *The future of the teaching profession: A new scenario set*, Centre for Strategic Education, Melbourne, http://www.cse.edu.au (accessed on 13 May 2020). [5]

Knox, J., B. Williamson and S. Bayne (2019), "Machine behaviourism: future visions of 'learnification' and 'datafication' across humans and digital technologies", *Learning, Media and Technology*, Vol. 45/1, pp. 31-45, http://dx.doi.org/10.1080/17439884.2019.1623251. [10]

Leadbeater, C. (2006), "The Future of Public Services: Personalised Learning", in *Personalising Education*, OECD Publishing, Paris, https://dx.doi.org/10.1787/9789264036604-8-en. [3]

Luckin, R. (2018), *Machine Learning and Human Intelligence: The Future of Education for the 21st Century.*, UCL Institute of Education Press, London. [30]

Luckin, R. et al. (2016), *Intelligence Unleashed An argument for AI in Education*, Pearson and UCL Knowledge Lab, https://edu.google.com/pdfs/Intelligence-Unleashed-Publication.pdf. [29]

Mesch, G. (2019), "Online and offline relationships", in *Educating 21st Century Children: Emotional Well-being in the Digital Age*, OECD Publishing, Paris, https://dx.doi.org/10.1787/11f6c5b4-en. [37]

Meynhardt, T. (2009), "Public value inside: What is public value creation?", *International Journal of Public Administration*, Vol. 32/3-4, pp. 192-219, http://dx.doi.org/10.1080/01900690902732632. [1]

Novak, M. (2012), *Predictions for Educational TV in the 1930s*, Smithsonian Magazine, https://www.smithsonianmag.com/history/predictions-for-educational-tv-in-the-1930s-107574983/ (accessed on 12 May 2020). [25]

OECD (2019), *PISA 2018 Results (Volume III): What School Life Means for Students' Lives*, PISA, OECD Publishing, Paris, https://dx.doi.org/10.1787/acd78851-en. [36]

OECD (2019), "Play!", *Trends Shaping Education Spotlights*, No. 18, OECD Publishing, Paris, https://dx.doi.org/10.1787/a4115284-en. [13]

OECD (2018), "A brave new world: Technology and education", *Trends Shaping Education Spotlights*, No. 15, OECD Publishing, Paris, https://dx.doi.org/10.1787/9b181d3c-en. [28]

OECD (2018), "Blended learning", in *Teachers as Designers of Learning Environments: The Importance of Innovative Pedagogies*, OECD Publishing, Paris, https://dx.doi.org/10.1787/9789264085374-7-en. [38]

OECD (2018), *Equity in Education: Breaking Down Barriers to Social Mobility*, PISA, OECD Publishing, Paris, https://dx.doi.org/10.1787/9789264073234-en. [18]

OECD (2017), *PISA 2015 Results (Volume V): Collaborative Problem Solving*, PISA, OECD Publishing, Paris, https://dx.doi.org/10.1787/9789264285521-en. [16]

OECD (2016), *Trends Shaping Education 2016*, OECD Publishing, Paris, https://dx.doi.org/10.1787/trends_edu-2016-en. [8]

Paniagua, A. and D. Istance (2018), *Teachers as Designers of Learning Environments: The Importance of Innovative Pedagogies*, Educational Research and Innovation, OECD Publishing, Paris, https://dx.doi.org/10.1787/9789264085374-en. [41]

Pellegrino, J. (2017), "Teaching, learning and assessing 21st century skills", in *Pedagogical Knowledge and the Changing Nature of the Teaching Profession*, OECD Publishing, Paris, https://dx.doi.org/10.1787/9789264270695-12-en. [42]

Selwyn, N. (2011), *Education and Technology: Key Issues and Debates*, Continuum, London and New York. [2]

Sivan, A. and R. Stebbins (2011), "Leisure education: definition, aims, advocacy, and practices – are we talking about the same thing(s)?", *World Leisure Journal*, Vol. 53/1, pp. 27-41, http://dx.doi.org/10.1080/04419057.2011.552216. [12]

The Institute for Ethical AI in Education (n.d.), *Interim Report Towards a shared Vision of Ethical AI in Education Contents*, The University of Buckingham. [32]

Theisens, H. (2016), "Hierarchies, networks and improvisation in education governance", in *Governing Education in a Complex World*, OECD Publishing, Paris, https://dx.doi.org/10.1787/9789264255364-5-en. [7]

Weidmann, B., D. Deming and H. School (2020), "Team Players: How Social Skills Improve Group Performance", *NBER Working Paper Series*, No. 27071, National Bureau of Economic Research, Cambridge, https://www.nber.org/papers/w27071.pdf (accessed on 12 May 2020). [15]

Williamson, B. (2016), "Silicon startup schools: technocracy, algorithmic imaginaries and venture philanthropy in corporate education reform", *Critical Studies in Education*, Vol. 59/2, pp. 218-236, http://dx.doi.org/10.1080/17508487.2016.1186710. [21]

Williamson, B. (2015), "Digital education governance: data visualization, predictive analytics, and 'real-time' policy instruments", *Journal of Education Policy*, Vol. 31/2, pp. 123-141, http://dx.doi.org/10.1080/02680939.2015.1035758. [20]

www.ingramcontent.com/pod-product-compliance
Lightning Source LLC
Chambersburg PA
CBHW081513200326
41518CB00015B/2483